GENERAL BILLY MITCHELL

by BOOTH MOONEY

General Billy Mitchell

illustrated with photographs

FOLLETT PUBLISHING COMPANY

Chicago ⊕ New York

COVER PAINTING BY HANK STALLWORTH

The author gratefully acknowledges the following organizations, which permitted the reproduction of photographs on the indicated pages: Culver Pictures, Inc., pp. 6, 100; European Picture Service, p. 150; Library of Congress, Frontispiece, pp. 25, 41, 49, 66, 68, 71, 81, 87, 93, 106, 113, 128, 133, 134, 141, 143, 154; National Archives, pp. 19, 146; Official U. S. Air Force Photo, p. 124.

Library of Congress Catalog Card Number: AC 67-21162

First Printing I

Follett Publishing Company
1010 West Washington Boulevard
Chicago, Illinois 60607

T/L 3340

GENERAL BILLY MITCHELL

Young Billy Mitchell.

CHAPTER ONE

WILLY MITCHELL was in a bad temper. He stormed
into the big house in downtown Milwaukee, Wisconsin, his five-year-old face rebellious and angry. His
dark eyes flashed as he faced his mother.

"Mother, I am not going to talk French any
more," he announced.

Harriet Mitchell looked down at the little figure.
"Why do you say that, son?" she asked quietly.

"The other boys laugh at me." Willy clenched
his fists. "They say I don't sound like an American
boy. They pull their noses at me and call me 'Froggie.'"

His mother placed a hand on his shoulder. "It
doesn't matter, Willy. You mustn't let such a little
thing upset you."

"I won't talk French," he said stubbornly.

Even as a child, Willy, later to become famous throughout the United States and much of the world as General Billy Mitchell, had a mind of his own.

It was true that when he was a small boy he spoke French better than English. This was not surprising. William Mitchell had been born in Nice, France, where his parents went for a long stay after their marriage. The boy's birth date was December 29, 1879.

Willy was three years old when the family moved back to the United States. In spite of the early trouble with his French accent, he soon showed that he was every inch an American boy.

In addition to the house in Milwaukee, John Lendrum Mitchell, Willy's father, owned a large farm called Meadowmere. The family spent much time there. It was a great place for a growing boy. There were fields to roam in, birds to watch, ponies to ride, cows to milk. The farm even had its own large private lake, which was wonderful for swimming and boating.

The Mitchell family grew until it contained seven children, two sons and five daughters. Willy was the oldest. He was the leader of the others in all their activities.

The children often went cruising on the lake in a flat-bottomed rowboat. Naturally, Willy was the captain. It never occurred to the others that anyone else would wear the captain's hat. Nor did it occur to Willy either, for he was not inclined to be modest about his abilities. In fact, he was something of a show-off, although not in an unpleasant way.

One day, when Willy was about ten years old, he and his brother, his sister Harriet and her friend, Eleanor Mercein, were taking a boat ride. As usual, the boat was leaking.

"Willy, what will happen when this boat sinks to the bottom?" Eleanor suddenly asked.

The captain looked at his passengers, his eyes sparkling. "I myself will carry you ashore," he proclaimed, "two at a time."

They never doubted that he would do it.

Billy, as the boy soon came to be called, had a wide range of interests, almost all of which came ahead of his school books. He loved horses and dogs. He was very fond of hunting and fishing and was an excellent swimmer. Before he was twelve years old, he started collecting and mounting specimens of Wisconsin birds.

His training in horsemanship started in early childhood. It was not always easy riding at first. One afternoon at the farm, he came in the house with his clothes badly mussed and his face shining with perspiration. He had been having a hard time with a horse.

"Mother, I just can't handle that beast," he grumbled.

Use of the word "can't" was not encouraged in the Mitchell household. His mother looked at him squarely. "Son," she said, "you just go on riding it until you can."

No wonder Billy started playing the thrilling, and sometimes dangerous, game of polo when he was only thirteen!

It was generally agreed in the family that Billy was like his grandfather, Alexander Mitchell, who at the age of twenty-one had emigrated from his native Scotland to the United States in the year 1839.

Alexander Mitchell had studied law and worked as a bank clerk in Scotland. On coming to the United States, he settled in Milwaukee. A man of great energy and with a natural knack for business, he prospered in his new home. He was a banker. When Billy was born, his grandfather was serving as president of the American Bankers Association. He also became head of a large railroad company and dealt profitably in the buying and selling of land. He served two terms in the United States House of Representatives.

Alexander Mitchell's only son, John, was wholly different from his father. He was a student and a humanitarian. He studied in Europe as a youth. When he returned home he showed little taste for business. He was a volunteer in the Union Army during the Civil War. After being honorably discharged because of an eye ailment, he turned to his interests in literature, languages, government, nature and scientific farming.

John Mitchell was married in 1878 to Harriet Danforth Becker of New York. She was a woman of great force and dignity, a wife who shared her husband's interests and a mother greatly devoted to her children.

Although Billy was like his grandfather in his restless, energetic nature, his father's concern with public affairs greatly influenced his own life. John Lendrum Mitchell served as president of the Milwaukee School Board and was one of the founders of the Agricultural College of the University of Wisconsin. He presented the college with scholarships for students of scientific farming. At Meadowmere he carried out experiments to improve crops and soils.

When Billy was ten, his father was elected to the

House of Representatives and then to the United States Senate. He was an idealistic man who favored disarmament as a step toward world peace. He advocated social legislation that was in advance of the times.

John Mitchell looked the part of a United States Senator. He had a beard that resembled a flowing waterfall. The glasses he wore did not hide the intelligent gleam of his eyes. When he spoke on behalf of the causes he favored, other senators listened. Billy was very proud of his father.

The boy attended a private school in Milwaukee and afterward graduated from Racine College, a preparatory school. He was not a great scholar, being more concerned with outdoor sports than with books, but he made grades that were respectable enough.

He did develop an early interest, which lasted all his life, in American history. His grandmother, Mrs. Alexander Mitchell, was one of three women who founded an organization to buy, restore, and make a national shrine of George Washington's Virginia home, Mount Vernon. Billy frequently visited Mount Vernon with his grandmother. She and the other ladies made George Washington a living person to him.

He also learned a great deal about military history. His father took the family on trips to Europe from time to time. Billy loved visiting the old battlefields with his father, who lectured the children on the meaning and consequences of the battles fought in these areas.

The trips to Europe came to an end in 1893. In that year there was a severe financial panic in the United States. Business concerns were forced into bankruptcy. Many thousands of people lost their jobs. Banking institutions throughout the United States were forced to close their doors.

The Mitchell family bank was among those that closed. Depositors of many banks lost heavily. But John Mitchell, with his high standards of honesty and integrity, was resolved that this should not happen to depositors in his family's bank.

"Our depositors have trusted us," he said firmly. "They shall not lose a single dollar."

Nor did they. The Mitchell bank was the only one in the Middle West which paid its depositors in full.

This was possible only because John Mitchell turned over his entire personal fortune to meet the bank's obligations. This cost him about one and one-third million dollars, taking everything he had except the farm at Meadowmere.

The Mitchells were poor now, at least by comparison with former times. The European tours were a thing of the past, and so was other free and easy spending. But there was no brooding over these matters.

The family turned the raising of thoroughbred horses at Meadowmere from a sport into a source of income. John Mitchell was in the Senate and, although senatorial salaries were not large in those days, the monthly checks were welcome.

Billy himself was little affected by the reversal in the family fortunes. He had always been most at home roaming the fields of the farm and engaging in the simple outdoor sports that cost little and were a great pleasure to him.

He went ahead to graduate from Racine College before he was sixteen. When he entered Columbia College (later to become George Washington University) in Washington, D.C., in 1895, he was the youngest student at the institution.

Life as a college student was most pleasant. Billy gave the necessary attention to his studies, but he was more interested in people and in games and sports. He went out for football and became quarterback and captain of the freshman team. He had brought with him to Washington a great array of golf clubs, tennis rackets, shotguns, fishing tackle, skates, and hockey equipment. He was generous in sharing these and became very popular among the other boys.

He had time, too, to explore the city of Washington. The family lived on Capitol Hill, in a house where the first Senate Office Building now stands. Billy wandered from there over the entire District of Columbia, led by his curiosity about people and places. He continued to go down to Mount Vernon in Virginia.

"America, its inspiring past and glowing future," in the words of his sister Ruth, who later wrote a book called *My Brother Bill*, "became the very warp and woof of Bill's own mind."

When summer came and college was not in session and neither was the Senate, the family returned happily to the farm in Wisconsin. Billy flourished there. The horses he loved were ready for riding. Meadowmere even had its own racetrack. He and his friends were sometimes allowed to drive the finest pacing and trotting horses hitched to what was called a sulky—an open, high-off-the-ground carriage.

It was all great fun.

From time to time the family went in the summer to a beach on the New Jersey coast. Billy learned sailing and quickly became an expert. During one summer he even went off by himself on a trip to Europe. He was especially impressed by the little nation of Switzerland, which, his father declared, might be held up as a model for all Europe.

Billy had been impressed by the natural beauty of Switzerland. His father had other things in mind when he addressed the graduating class of 1897 at the college his son was attending.

"I have had a dream," Senator Mitchell told the graduates, "an iridescent dream. The nations of Europe do not differ more radically in races, religion, speech, and local customs than do the Cantons of Switzerland. Why might not these nations of Europe federate themselves under a similar system—one which centuries of experience have proved to be more beneficial and more stable than the forms of government under which they live?"

The Senator's dream was of peace in the world, good will among peoples. But this dream was not yet to be realized.

Billy enjoyed his college days, although he was hardly a model student. His youthful energy at times led him into mischief. His friends at Columbia College followed him as his brothers and sisters and the neighboring children had followed him at Meadowmere. If on occasion he led them into trouble, he was quick to assume his full share of the blame.

By this time the young man who had resented being called "Froggie" had reached the full height he was to attain—five feet, nine inches. Rather slight of stature, he was a handsome youngster. His light hair, with a wave he detested, was parted in the middle. His dark, expressive eyes drew the attention of everyone he met. His nose was a bit long, but he had an easy, engaging smile that won friends for him wherever he went.

All was going well for Billy Mitchell, the college student. Then, when he was eighteen years old and in his third year of college, the United States went to war, and his life was changed suddenly and for all time.

CHAPTER TWO

In Cuba, less than one hundred miles from the Florida keys, the people had risen up against the tyrannical rule of Spain. The United States was sympathetic with the uprising. The battleship *Maine* was sent to stand by in Havana Harbor.

U.S. Navy Commodore George Dewey was in command of a fleet sailing in Asiatic waters. He had secret orders to take the Philippine Islands if war broke out between the United States and Spain.

On February 15, 1898, the *Maine* was blown up by an explosion. The big ship sank in Havana Harbor with a loss of 266 lives.

Spain was blamed for the tragedy, although it was never fully proved that she was responsible. Great agitation began in the United States in favor of going to war against that nation. Two New York City newspapers, in heated competition, tried to outdo each other in whipping up war sentiment among the people. Every day they and other papers published news stories, many of them of questionable authenticity, about the cruelty of the Spaniards toward the people of Cuba.

"Remember the *Maine!*" screamed the headlines.

Billy Mitchell fully accepted the popular picture of an oppressed people rising against tyrants. On the April day that the war was declared against Spain, he sat tense and silent in the visitors' gallery of the Senate chamber. He was afraid that his father, who had spoken so often in opposition to armed conflict between nations, would vote against the declaration of war.

The wreck of the *Maine* in the harbor at Havana, Cuba.

He need not have worried. Senator John Mitchell was among those who had become convinced that the Spanish forces had deliberately blown up the *Maine* with no regard for the lives of those aboard. His vote was cast with that of other senators for war with Spain.

Billy ran home and started packing. The war to him meant high adventure. He was determined to enlist in the army at once. Since he was only eighteen, he must have the consent of his parents. This they gave, although with reluctance. Billy was so young, his mother thought with pain and anxiety. But she knew that this was something her son, now almost a man, was determined to do.

Milwaukee was home to the Mitchells, and it was there that Billy went to enlist in the 1st Wisconsin Infantry Regiment of the Wisconsin National Guard. As a private soldier, he underwent three weeks of very rigorous training. Then his regiment was ready to be off on the way to war.

The new soldiers paraded through the streets of Milwaukee on their march to the railroad station. Many people stood on the sidewalks to cheer them as they passed by.

Billy marched proudly with the others. He felt that he was truly a soldier. There was a swing to his walk. Suddenly he saw in the crowd two faces he knew well: those of his childhood friend, Eleanor Mercein, and her mother. They waved frantically at Billy, and he gave a shy wave and a smile in return.

From the train transporting the Wisconsin regiment to an army camp in Florida, Billy wrote his mother:

"As I write people are cheering, flags waving, and bands playing all along the road, one continued goodby. We got off the train at Nashville to get some exercise and marched a few miles. Everyone thought us regulars on account of our equipment and fine drilling. Well, we *are* regulars now, having been sworn into the U.S. Service."

A week after his arrival at the Tampa camp, Billy was summoned by his commanding officer and ordered to proceed to Washington. A family friend, General Adolphus W. Greely, chief of the Army Signal Corps, had recommended him for a commission as an officer.

The youthful second lieutenant was assigned to a Signal Corps company being organized at Washington barracks. He did not like the idea of leaving his Wisconsin friends. He had hoped to be with them in Cuba before long.

But, as he told himself, "Orders are orders," and off he went to Washington.

While he was there, one day an emergency call came to the barracks. Men were to be sent immediately to help local police in subduing a group of soldiers who had left their train in the capital while on the way to an army camp. These men, about seventy-five of then, had taken over the kitchen and bar of a hotel near the railroad station. They were eating and drinking and smashing up the place. They had thrown out policemen trying to restore order.

Billy immediately asked that he be allowed to take men to bring in the rioters. His superior officer hesitated. Lieutenant Mitchell was so young! But finally he was told to go ahead.

Billy gathered fourteen enlisted men to go along. Then he commandeered a trolley car and told the motorman to get to the hotel as fast as he could. On reaching there, the young officer lined up his armed men along the curb facing the building. The place was surrounded by policemen. Shouts of revelry came from inside.

The police captain told Billy that the soldiers were very dangerous. He thought that anybody who went in would probably be set upon and badly hurt or even killed.

Billy placed men at each of the two doors leading from the hotel. He told them not to shoot but that if any of the soldiers tried to escape they should be knocked down and arrested. Then he and his former college mate, Robert Sterrett, left their weapons behind and went inside.

The place was a shambles. Several of the soldiers were behind the bar mixing drinks for their companions. Occasionally a man would toss a bottle at the large mirror, already broken, on the wall. The sound of crashing glass brought a roar of delight from the others.

Billy himself was so amused that he could hardly stop laughing long enough to shout, "Attention!"

The military command brought all but two or three of the men stiffly erect. The shouting died away. The first sergeant came forward to assist in leading his men outside where they were lined up for a roll call.

"I decided to march them all the way to Washington Barracks, three miles," Billy Mitchell wrote later. "At my request, the captain of police got a couple of firemen to accompany me, with buckets and wrenches for the hydrants, not only to furnish the men with drinking water, but to throw water over those who seemed to need a little bracing up. It was a terribly hot day, and when they arrived at the barracks, they were practically all sober. I halted them under the shade of the trees and gave them water, then reported their presence to the officer of the guard, who took charge of them."

Billy found the men had some excuse for their unsoldierly conduct. Their first sergeant told him that their officers had gone on ahead in railroad parlor cars without properly providing for their men. The soldiers had been practically without food for two days, the first sergeant said. When they saw the hotel across from the station, he was unable to hold them.

Billy had shown on this occasion the same sort of leadership that he had displayed in the childish games at Meadowmere. He was a man, even though a quite young one, who acted coolly and quickly in an emergency. General Greely, head of the Signal Corps and the officer who had recommended him for a commission, sent for the lieutenant to extend his personal compliments on the way he had handled matters. It was an excellent beginning for the young officer's army career.

Soon Billy was back in Florida, this time at Camp Cuba Libre—Free Cuba—near Jacksonville. He assumed the post of second in command of the signal company to which he was assigned.

The Signal Corps had the responsibility of putting in place, maintaining, and operating telephone and telegraph equipment for the army. Billy took his work with great seriousness. He learned the code used on the telegraph lines and also taught himself to use a typewriter.

Within weeks after his arrival at Camp Cuba Libre he wrote his parents: "I have had charge of all the telephone lines of all the camps for nearly a month and also the telegraph. I know the signal code perfectly. I have been asked if I would like to take charge of a regular signal company of about 22 men."

So the young officer had his own command. At a review of troops the commanding officer of the camp commended him in the presence of other officers for his outstanding work—"and he's an old regular army

Lt. Mitchell (extreme left, standing) with fellow Signal Corps officers at Jacksonville, Fla., 1898.

man," Billy told his mother with pride.

He also said, "I like this kind of work very much and find that it is doing me as much good as college would this fall."

Billy had time for play as well as work. He was a gay companion, well liked by the men under his command and respected by his fellow-officers. His Grandmother Mitchell owned an estate, Villa Alexandria, only a few miles from camp. He spent much of his off-duty time visiting there.

He bought a fine, high-spirited horse. "No one else in camp can ride her, but I can do anything with her," he reported.

Often he and his friend, Bob Sterrett, would ride together to his grandmother's place. They would leave camp in a very military fashion. Sterrett as an enlisted orderly rode a little to the rear until they were out of Jacksonville and in the country. Then their military pose fell away. They were a couple of boys together, laughing and racing their horses until they reached Villa Alexandria. There they would enjoy themselves swimming in the fine pool, eating pies, drinking milk, and playing games.

Billy also often went riding with another officer, Captain Howard Giddings. He taught his horse to kick the captain's horse, causing the animal to bolt every time Billy drew alongside. It was an exciting game to them, although Captain Giddings confessed that he was nearly as frightened as his horse was. Billy was never content to ride sedately along the road. He was forever sending his mount over fences and across ditches.

He worked hard and played hard, but all the while he was hoping and planning to be sent to Cuba. During that spring and summer of 1898, with Commodore Dewey winning victories over the Spanish fleet and American soldiers landing in Cuba, Billy Mitchell felt he was standing on the sidelines. It was not a feeling he liked at all.

"Am anxiously waiting to get on the transport to Cuba," he said in a letter to the family. "We will operate all the telegraph, telephone, and railroad lines and will have a good chance not only to see the country but will have absolute charge of certain sections."

But the order to "get on the transport" did not come. When Spain finally gave up the fight in August and asked for peace, Billy wrote, "I am very much disgusted that affairs have taken this turn."

His father advised him to resign his commission and come home to enter the banking business. Billy gave serious consideration to this proposal. He liked the army very much and he was proud of the responsibility that had been placed on him. But none of this was enough unless he could get into action. If only he would be sent to Cuba!

"I'm going to get there some way or other," he told his father stoutly. "I've been waiting all summer to get a chance to do something and have not had it, and think it would be a shame to go home now. There would be no self-satisfaction in going home and would look sort of funny too."

Besides, he added, "I am in command of a company now and have the best company here for any kind of work."

He was not ready to go home. His pride in his organization showed that he was a born military officer. This worked two ways, for men under his command were always devoted to Billy Mitchell.

The summer passed, fall came, and still he fretted at Camp Cuba Libre. Then at last, late in November, his company received orders to set sail for Cuba. They were to serve in the Army of Occupation to bring order back to the war-torn island.

Billy Mitchell spent Christmas Eve in Havana. He would be nineteen years old in a few days.

He wrote his father that day: "This is a better Christmas Eve in one way than I expected. I did not think we would be in Cuba. We are situated on a high bluff overlooking the sea. As I sit here, the company is lined up for retreat, the sky is streaked in red, white and blue in the West, with a few stars showing. It truly looks like our flag."

On New Year's Day he witnessed the formal surrender of the Spanish forces in front of the Governor General's Palace in Havana. As soon as he landed in Cuba he had acquired a fine gray horse, and he rode the steed to the scene of the surrender ceremony.

"Our men were drawn up in a hollow square all around the court, while the Spaniards were lined up in front of the Palace," he reported. "I was right in the Palace all the time watching the ceremonies.

"At precisely 12:02 by the clock on the Palace, the Spanish flag came down and ours went up. As we stood there with bared heads, it was an impressive event. Our men stood like statues while the Spaniards flinched and were very nervous."

The band played the "Star-Spangled Banner," then a Spanish melody, and the Spanish officers and soldiers walked down to board a ship that lay at the wharf. As the Spanish steamer came up the bay, a huge American flag was raised on the wreck of the *Maine*.

Soon afterward Billy received official instructions regarding his first assignment in Cuba. His heart beat faster as he read the orders. He thrilled to the foreign names of the cities:

"The orders directing you to proceed to Gibara and thence to Holguin with men and materials to assist in the construction of telegraph lines place under your charge an important work upon the completion of which telegraphic communications will be established between Havana and Santiago de Cuba.

"You will organize native laborers who will cut the poles and place them on the line. Care should be taken to have the poles placed firmly in the ground and the line solidly built, and to provide for the welfare of the men under your command. See that they are camped in healthy locations and not unnecessarily exposed to sun and rain."

He was in Cuba and he had a job to do. Lieutenant William Mitchell was a very happy young man.

CHAPTER THREE

THE SPANIARDS were gone from Cuba, but the island was not a serene and happy place. The rebellious natives had become accustomed to fighting. Now some of them became bandits and turned their guns against the American Army of Occupation.

The island had been ruined by years of warfare. Large bands of ragged, hungry Cubans set upon villages and towns to loot and rob. Smallpox and yellow fever raged among the populace. Soon many American soldiers were falling victim to these diseases.

Billy Mitchell plunged with eager zest into the work he had been assigned to do. Early in February he set sail for the town of Gibara. He took with him forty men and a doctor and necessary supplies and pack animals. His orders called for him to proceed by rail from Gibara to the town of Holguin. That was the starting point for the telegraph line he had been instructed to build.

When the steamship reached Gibara, the captain told Mitchell to unload his men, equipment and animals on a smaller boat for landing. This craft looked to Mitchell as if it might sink any moment. He refused to board it, calling the captain's attention to a big fine flatboat in the harbor.

Mitchell reported in a letter to his family what happened next: "He then called his men to put us off, telling me he was captain of the ship and so on. He thought as we were such a small detachment he could bluff us and save money as the big boat cost $50 a trip. So I just issued ammunition to my men and ran him and his men to the stern of the ship, then went ashore and ordered the big flatboat to be sent out—which was done."

For the young officer it was all in the day's work. He felt it was always his responsibility to see that men under his command were treated properly.

Work was started immediately on laying the telegraph line. Twelve miles of line were put into place in just two days. Then there was a delay because it was learned that a band of 3,000 insurgent Cubans were encamped on the route they meant to take. Mitchell was advised to wait a day or so until they moved on.

"We will push the line with all possible speed," Mitchell assured his commanding officer, Colonel H. H. Dunwoody.

He found time to marvel at the many brilliantly colored birds he saw in the tropical land. They caused him to remember his collection of birds back in Milwaukee. Less pleasant were the snakes he and his men encountered in the jungle, among them boa constrictors twelve feet or more in length. Everything was new and strange, and Mitchell reported all he saw in the frequent letters he sent to his family.

One spring night he wrote from an obscure village named Puerto Padre: "I came last night with one man to reconnoiter for the line. We were the first Americans to come into the town. This place is the home of all bandit business. We took 32 rifles away from them. We didn't have much trouble. One colonel was a little ugly about giving up a gun and machete he had on his person, but I soon persuaded him with my old six-shooter."

This was adventure. Lieutenant Mitchell loved every minute of it. He had learned to speak Spanish fluently and was able to talk freely with the natives. He spent several months in the interior of Cuba. For a full month he was on his own with his men, completely out of touch with headquarters in Havana. Even when his father and mother, at different times, visited the island, he was unable to see them.

By the end of May he had completed his assigned task. He and his men had built 138 miles of telegraph line. It was more than any other detachment of the Signal Corps then in Cuba had constructed.

"It has been a pretty big strain on my men," he reported, "and they are pretty well tired out."

He wrote an official review of the work that had been done. It drew this commendation from General Greely, chief of the Signal Corps: "It is a very creditable report, and indicates that this officer, despite his youth, is a man of ability, energy, and intelligence. I have seen few reports giving so much information in clear cut form on a technical subject of such range."

Mitchell was appointed assistant signal officer on the staff of General Fitzhugh Lee, who was in command of the American forces in Cuba. This meant that he was stationed in Havana. His life there was about as different as could be imagined from his experiences in the interior of Cuba. The Cuban capital was gay with parties and dancing. The handsome lieutenant was much in demand. He enjoyed it all, but he was not satisfied.

He wanted to go to the Philippine Islands.

Even when he was still engaged in building the telegraph lines, he had fretted to be assigned to the Philippines. After American military forces had moved into that area, a new insurrection had broken out and at times there was heavy fighting. Mitchell longed to get into the action.

"You don't know how much I want to go to the Philippines," he told his family. "Can't something be done to get me assigned there?"

His mother immediately made it clear, in a letter addressed to "My dear boy," that his father would not use his influence in Washington to bring about such an assignment.

"I saw General Greely today," she wrote, "and he told me you would remain in Cuba, and would be sent to various places as required. He said you were showing a great deal of ability in your work and they were very much pleased with you, that you seemed to get on well with the men and that you made an excellent officer.

"We could not ask them to have any assignment for you, as it seems to disgust them at the War Department to have favors asked, and one reason why you stand so well is that you have taken the assignments without question and no relative has been try-ing to push you."

Billy Mitchell loved his parents and was ex-tremely reluctant to go against their wishes. But he felt that he was a grown man and had proved himself as an officer. He must somehow get to the Philip-pines. He made formal application for a transfer.

"I believe that I would go as a private if I can get a chance," he told his father. "If you want me to resign after that I will, and either go in business or go back to college in some law school."

Reluctantly his parents withdrew their objec-tions. In August Mitchell received orders to leave for the Philippine Islands.

"I consider it my duty to go," he wrote his moth-er. "I am not in this business for a good time. Now I have a good chance to work in the field, and know I can carry it through in a satisfactory manner."

Before proceeding to the Philippines he was granted leave for a short visit to the United States. His father met him in Washington, the rest of the fam-ily being in Europe. Senator Mitchell was well pleased with the effect of military life on his son.

"His army experience up to date has been the making of him, physically and mentally," the Senator told his wife in a letter. "He stands straight and talks straight, and I may say entertainingly. The impression he has made here on everybody is very favorable."

The lieutenant created the same kind of impression in Milwaukee, his old home, where he proceeded from Washington. Handsome in his officer's uniform, smiling and high-spirited, he was made much of by old friends and new. Mrs. Mercein, the family friend who had watched him parade along the streets of Milwaukee when he first joined the army, wrote Mrs. Mitchell that her son "seems the perfect type of the ideal American soldier."

He had a fine time, but Billy Mitchell never forgot for a moment that he was headed for service in the Philippines. It was a glad day for him on October 5, 1899, when he found himself aboard one of three ships filled with troops on their way to Manila.

The voyage was a long one, lasting twenty-seven days, broken by a stopover in the fascinating Hawaiian city of Honolulu. On the ship Mitchell used his time purposefully to read everything he could put his hands on about the Philippine Islands and the people who lived there. He also gave a series of lectures on engineering and the principles of signaling to other officers on his ship.

As the vessel approached its destination it met with heavy seas. Every movable article had to be fastened down to keep it from rolling about.

"I put a can of pears on the washstand last night," Mitchell wrote gleefully to his father. "In the middle of the night the ship gave an extra roll and spilled the whole sticky outfit right in my roommate's face. As he was asleep, he almost went crazy."

The Philippines had been ceded to the United States by Spain at the end of the war between the two countries. As the people in the Philippines saw this transaction, they had simply exchanged one master for another. They had been fighting to win their independence from Spain. It was no comfort to them to find themselves owned by the United States instead.

Still seeking independence, a large part of the Filipino army had resorted to guerrilla warfare under the leadership of General Emilio Aguinaldo. Bitter fighting had been going on for months. The civilian population as well as the armed forces suffered from its effects. The American army had been victorious in the field, but strong pockets of resistance remained.

Mitchell was promptly assigned to General Arthur MacArthur and, to his great joy, given an independent command. To him, as to most Americans at the time, there was no question of right or wrong in the war against the Filipinos. They were the enemy of the United States and must be conquered.

"There is going to be a large battle in a few days," he informed his family. "This is business right through."

And he added: "Nothing is going to stop my men no matter what happens."

The Signal Corps had a tough job in the Philippines. It was necessary for the field telegraph to follow close to the firing line so that the general at headquarters could be given full and immediate information about developments. The telegraph lineman's first responsibility was to work, not to fight—but he had to be ready to fight at any time.

Soon after his arrival, Mitchell reported to the folks at home: "We are advancing along the railroad track from Manila to Dagugan, a distance of 130 miles. The night was quite dark and everything was a flame of fire along our front. We ran lines to our right front, left and center; so that all General Mac-Arthur had to do was to sit at the instrument."

He gloried in action: "Our next scrap was at Mavalang, where I got our line into the rebel trenches ahead of the troops. The Insurrectos ran, blowing up a big railroad bridge. We had a pretty good scrap there. We always have our telegraph line *there* and working wherever the troops go; and I go up and down the line organizing our work."

In this kind of fast-moving operation through jungle country, transportation was of vital importance. Mitchell found that the principal modes of transportation available to him were water buffalo and trotting bulls. The water buffalo was a large black animal with a tremendous hump on his back and great horns measuring as much as eight feet across. To his delight, Mitchell discovered that the trotting bulls could move as fast as an ordinary horse and were capable of covering great distances without tiring.

Naturally, if a horse was to be had the young officer would soon acquire one for his own use. He got a fine native pony—"very fast," he reported, and "with a great lot of spirit." In addition to the water buffalo, used for very heavy hauling, he had pack ponies. One of them was no more than three feet tall. Mitchell thought he looked more like a large mouse than anything else.

It was a strenuous life. He and his men often went through rice fields with water up to their waists and through forests and thickets of bamboo. In some of the rivers they had to cross, the currents were so swift that men would be carried away and drowned if they were washed off rafts and lost their hold on

A Signal Corps camp near Manila.

ropes they had stretched across the swirling waters.

Mitchell himself often swam the alligator-infested rivers to put the first rope across. He was never willing to send men under his command against danger that he would not face.

"Am enjoying this very much," he wrote joyfully. "Have good ponies, men who will follow me anywhere and are good shots and good telegraph operators, good cooks and good everything, the best scouts in the business."

The work of scouts was of great importance in

the unknown jungle country. Mitchell himself had
the benefit of association with one of the most expert
scouts in the American army, Colonel Frederick Funston. This man, who came from Kansas, held a commission in the volunteers. He had fought in Cuba
against the Spaniards even before the United States
declared war on Spain. He had considerable military
experience.

Colonel Funston regarded the closed minds of
many regular army officers with considerable con-
tempt. He exerted great influence over young Mitchell and helped to shape his thinking on many matters.

During his year and a half in the Philippines,
Mitchell supervised the building of the longest stretch
of telegraph mileage in the entire network of 16,000
miles of wire and cables constructed by the army. He
also extended his range of knowledge by learning the
rudiments of electricity and by study of the science
of military tactics. At the age of twenty-one he had
become a mature, experienced officer, wise in leadership and capable of remarkable feats of physical en-
durance.

Besides work and study, he found time for his
favorite sport of hunting. Fierce wild boars roamed
the countryside, and he was enthralled by hunting

them on horseback. On one day he rode a pony seventeen hours without dismounting, then changed ponies and rode two hours more.

"We were hunting all the time," he proudly told his family.

He also learned to use a bow and arrow in the manner of the Filipinos. The native archer picked up the bow with his bare feet while lying on his back and then released the arrow from that position. Mitchell became expert at this odd art.

He learned that life in the raw jungle made men remarkably self-sufficient. After he and his men had been in the field for a long time, it seemed there was hardly anything that was impossible for them to do. They had no watches, so they made a sun dial to use in the daylight hours and an hourglass fashioned from two bottles for use at night.

"We can make anything," Mitchell boasted, "from gunpowder to telegraph instruments if necessary, and we always seem to beat the difficulties in the end by simple hustle."

All the while U.S. military forces were aiming their efforts at capturing General Aguinaldo. He was the center of continued resistance, and it was felt that his capture would result in hostilities being brought to an end soon after.

But General Aguinaldo was most elusive. He was forever slipping away from the Americans when they thought they had him safely surrounded. Once, Mitchell wrote, it was rumored that he had slipped through the American lines disguised as a Chinese. The natives hid and protected the general, either because they believed in his cause or were frightened by his fierce guerrilla fighters.

Mitchell of course had hopes that it would fall to his fate to capture the wily Aguinaldo. He sought and obtained permission to organize a unit of native scouts to gather information about the hiding places of the scattered bands of guerrillas. This idea was highly successful. Mitchell's scouts immediately started bringing in valuable information regarding the revolutionary groups.

Their value was proved by an important incident that took place in May, 1900. For several days Mitchell's camp had been attacked by hidden snipers. Mitchell decided this must be stopped. He went into a nearby village and gained information from men there about where the guerrilla headquarters was located. He checked this information by making three night reconnaissances with two other men. The information proved to be accurate, and Mitchell prepared to act.

Leaving his own men to guard the camp, he borrowed fifteen men and a young officer from a regular army encampment nearby. The detachment advanced around midnight to an open field opposite the enemy camp. Charging across the field, they took the guerrillas by surprise and captured their camp without the loss of a single man.

Mitchell quickly discovered that the leader of the rebels was a Captain Mendoza. This man was known to be adjutant general of what was left of Aguinaldo's army. He was an important prize, having in his possession documents that gave valuable information about Aguinaldo's military organization.

In writing his father about the capture, Mitchell said, "Mendoza surrendered to me personally and his whole outfit with their arms. I have Mendoza's only side arm, a thirty-eight caliber pistol."

He went ahead in the next few weeks to capture more than seventy insurgent flags, seven official seals, and a great quantity of orders affecting the insurgent forces.

Mendoza's surrender intensified the hunt for Aguinaldo. But that slippery individual still managed to avert capture. Mitchell tried to get special permission to go after the rebel general, but General MacArthur thought his youth made him unsuitable for the assignment. The responsibility was given instead to Funston, and Mitchell received leave to go to the United States.

His orders called for him to proceed by way of the Orient and Europe. He was in the Orient in March, 1901, when word was flashed to the world that Funston had captured Aguinaldo.

Summing up his experience in the Philippines in a thoughtful letter to his father, Mitchell wrote: "I have found that I have accomplished more in these nearly two years than in all the rest put together. It has been to my liking and mixed with plenty of outdoor exercise, with horses and guns which I think I shall always have to have in some form or another."

He had about made up his mind to leave the military service. His father had not sought reelection to the Senate, and the family was again living in Milwaukee. Mitchell's plan was to go there and enter the banking business.

Instead, he received a commission as first lieutenant in the regular army and was sent off on an adventure in Alaska that was exactly to his liking.

CHAPTER FOUR

WHILE BILLY MITCHELL was soldiering in Cuba and the Philippines, great things had been happening in the Territory of Alaska. That northern land had been purchased by the United States from the Czar of Russia in 1867. Few white men went there until vast gold deposits were discovered at the end of the nineteenth century. The hope of quick riches brought thousands of fortune hunters pouring into Alaska to stake mining claims.

Once in Alaska, they were cut off from the civilized world during the winter months. Even in the summer, communications were slow and uncertain. The Signal Corps had been successful in laying down an underwater cable from Seattle, Washington, to the Alaskan port of Valdez. But efforts to construct an overland telegraph line in the wild country had made little progress.

It was to find out the reasons for the delay and how to overcome it that General Greely sent Mitchell to Alaska in the summer of 1901. He knew that the young lieutenant had as much knowledge about building telegraph lines under difficult conditions as any man in the country.

Mitchell spent several weeks covering the vast territory, much of which was unexplored. He soon concluded he had hit on a way of speeding up the job that had to be done.

Up until that time, work had been attempted only during the brief summer months. Even then, the workers were hampered by deep mud and vicious insects. In the winter the cold was so intense that no one had thought of carrying on the work then. This was wrong, Mitchell decided.

"Very little will be accomplished if we attempt to transport material through this area in the summer," he argued. "A pack horse could carry only 200 pounds fifteen or twenty miles a day. But in the winter these same animals could carry one thousand or two thousand pounds over the frozen snow for even greater distances.

"The thing to do," he declared, after completing

Signal Corps officers and men before departure to work on Alaskan overland telegraphic line.

his survey, "is to work through the winter getting the material out—the wire, insulators, poles, food supplies, and forage for the animals. Then we can construct the lines in the summer, when we could dig holes in the ground and set telegraph poles."

He took his plan to Washington. Greely was pleased with it and told him to go ahead. In the fall Mitchell returned to Alaska.

He made his headquarters at Fort Egbert, near

the town of Eagle City in the Klondike region. The first telegraph line would run from there to Valdez. That was where the submarine cable from the United States ended.

The distance was about 400 miles through the wilderness. There were no trails over the mountains which must be crossed. A survey would have to be made to see just where the lines would be placed.

Taking a man named Emmet with him, Mitchell set out by dog sled. They traveled light. Sometimes they slept in a hole in the snow with the dogs lying on top of them to keep them warm. The temperature over the snow-covered land often went down to sixty degrees below zero.

One day, as they were traveling across a small river called the Tokio, their sleds broke through the treacherous surface of ice. The river, fed by warm springs, had layer on layer of ice with about three feet of water between the layers. In an instant both men were wet up to their shoulders.

The moment they came out of the water and were exposed to the frigid air their moccasins and trousers froze. Unless they could do something they would very quickly freeze to death.

Emmet managed to get his sled ashore, but Mitchell's dogs were still floundering in the water.

As his lead dog, a fine animal named Pointer, struggled toward the shore, Mitchell saw a dry tree leaning over the river.

"Get that tree, Emmet!" he shouted. "We've got to have a fire."

As he reached the shore, he saw his companion grab a double-bitted ax and go for the tree. Mitchell turned his dogs loose from the harness. Moving as fast as he could, he grabbed two candles from his sled and lighted them with matches he carried in a shotgun case to keep them dry. Then he jumped into the water to keep from freezing.

With Emmet's first stroke the ax handle, made brittle by the bitter cold, broke in two. The man looked helplessly at the pieces.

"I'm beginning to freeze!" he cried.

"Jump in the water," Mitchell ordered. "I'll get my ax."

His own ax handle broke when he had the tree only halfway chopped through. Mitchell felt the cold eating into his body. Again he jumped into the water. As he did so, Emmet came out of the river and got another ax from his sled. He tackled the tree once more. He got it down this time and in a moment had stripped off the branches.

Using the candles to ignite the branches, the

two men quickly built a roaring fire. Soon men and dogs, warm and hungry, had a fine meal prepared by Mitchell. But it was a close call.

They spent the night beside the river and hit the trail again the next morning. Through the hard Alaskan winter they went on to the coast. Mitchell had the satisfaction of knowing that they had traveled the entire route over which the telegraph line was to be built.

The trip back to Fort Egbert was easier, since they were able to follow the trail they had broken on the way out. On the return journey Mitchell fell in with the Middlefork Indians. Their chief, Joseph, later became one of his great friends and companions. Chief Joseph, although a young man of only thirty years, was the leader of thirteen families of Middle-forks, who were outstanding hunters, trappers and fishermen.

Reaching Fort Egbert, Mitchell planned to get his men to work as soon as possible. In January of 1902, the group headed south. They surveyed the telegraph route and transported poles and supplies to be stored along the way for future use. By the end of the winter a right-of-way had been cut to the Tanana River, 150 miles from Fort Egbert.

As spring approached and the ice in the streams

showed signs of breaking up, Mitchell led his party back to Fort Egbert. The sled dogs were put in the corral for the summer. Ducks began to fly from the south, thousands and thousands of them. At last, in May, the ice in the Yukon River began to break. This was a spectacle that Mitchell watched in wonder and awe.

"A great bend in the river here," he wrote later, "has as its background an enormous mass of rock called Eagle Cliff, against which the ice piles up for more than 100 feet. Great cakes from five to ten feet thick grind and crash together with a noise like an artillery preparation for attack, for two or three days. Every day the river moved more and more and finally was clear."

The short summer had come to Alaska. The days were long and bright with sunshine. Wild flowers sprang up almost overnight, covering the ground. Mosquitoes also sprang up in great masses. The men grew beards as a protection against their savage bites.

Mitchell pushed himself and his men hard. During that summer they placed a telegraph line in operation from Fort Egbert to the Tanana. At that point the line was connected with a line another working party had laid from Valdez.

But the job was not finished. A second line must be built from Fort Egbert to Fort Gibbon, running through completely unexplored wilderness. Part of the route lay along the Goodpaster River. No white man had ever traveled down this river.

Mitchell set out just after New Year's Day, 1903, to scout the new route. He was accompanied by a man named "Dutch" De Haus. Three days later they were joined by Chief Joseph. The chief was reluctant to go with them.

"May never see my own people again," he muttered. "We go into the country of the bad Indians."

Yet he was with the other two as they started down the Goodpaster River, a beautiful stream with trees lining its banks. The white man had called on him in the name of friendship, and he could not refuse.

It was a bitterly cold January. Mitchell had trouble with his long nose, the tip of which was constantly being frozen. To protect it, he put a little piece of snowshoe rabbit fur on the end of his nose. The hairs of this fur stuck out about an inch and a half, and the piece was held to his nose by the congealed moisture from his face. He looked rather odd, but his nose no longer was in danger of being frozen.

The men traveled on snowshoes, covering about fifteen miles a day in deep snow. Mitchell insisted that they stay within sight of one another. He knew the danger of a man falling in the snow and giving up to the intense cold.

On the seventh day out, he noticed with concern that Dutch was beginning to fall behind. As he and Joseph rounded a turn in the river, he looked back and did not see the other man. He and the Indian exchanged worried looks.

"Joe, I'll have to go back and find him," Mitchell said.

"Yes," Joseph agreed instantly. "Cold can kill."

Mitchell looked ahead. He saw a dry tree sticking over the bank of the river.

"Get to that tree and build a fire," he said. "I have an idea we're going to need one."

He went as fast as he could back around the bend of the river. He had gone about 150 yards when he saw Dutch lying in the snow. He approached the man.

"Dutch, get up from there this moment!" he snapped. "Why didn't you keep up with us?"

Dutch looked up at him with dull eyes. "I was so tired," he explained. "I have to lie down and take a rest."

"Well, get up!"

"I don't believe I can move," Dutch said. "Anyway, I'm perfectly comfortable."

Mitchell took no time to argue. He could tell that the man's circulation already was slowing up, and freezing would soon follow. He had to arouse him. He jumped on the recumbent form with his snowshoes. He kicked Dutch in the chest and stomach.

"Get up!" he cried. "Get up and fight!"

Finally he got Dutch to his feet, but he had to push and drag the man along the trail. Going around the turn, he saw that his Indian friend had a fine fire going.

Dutch also saw the fire. It brought him to life. He ran for the fire and jumped squarely into it. The other two rushed to drag him out. Fortunately, he was not injured. One snowshoe and one moccasin were partly burned, but not beyond repair.

Mitchell and Joseph gave Dutch great quantities of hot tea and finally got him warmed up. All three enjoyed a hearty lunch and set out again. But now Mitchell ordered Dutch to stay ahead of the dog sleds carrying their supplies. That way they could always keep him in sight.

A few days later, without further incident other than the continuous struggle against the cold, the three men reached the mouth of the Goodpaster River. There they found an Indian villiage consisting of a dozen log cabins. Several of the Indians had some knowledge of English because they had journeyed far to trade their furs. But they had never before seen a white man in their village.

They were friendly, but they wanted to know why Mitchell was there. He told them that he was a soldier chief and that he was putting up a "talk string." That is what the Indians called the telegraph line. Mitchell also explained that the line would be helpful to them because, as it went straight from one point to another, it would always make an excellent winter trail available.

But why, the Indians asked, had he brought an Indian of another tribe with him? The stranger might find out things they did not wish him to know.

"Just as I am a soldier chief, Joseph is an Indian chief," Mitchell replied. "He is my friend and companion. We hunt together and fish together. He did not want to come, but I needed him to help me."

The Goodpaster Indians were satisfied with this explanation. They understood friendship. They made the visitors welcome, and all of them smoked and talked together.

All through the winter Mitchell made long survey trips from Fort Egbert to the Tanana River and back. He took time out during one stay at the fort to become a member of the Society of Arctic Brothers.

This was a secret organization, established just for fun, of men who had spent at least one winter in the North and thus were entitled to be called "sourdoughs."

In the initiation ceremony, the new member had to walk barefoot in the snow at thirty-five degrees below zero. Then he was rolled around in the snow for several minutes by his laughing friends. After that he was brought under shelter, given a warmed spiced drink, and formally made a member of the Society. It was just what Mitchell liked—rough companionship with men who, like him, had withstood the rigors of the North Country.

But he never neglected his serious business. As spring neared, he was determined to complete the telegraph line during the summer months. He established an advance base at the head of the Goodpaster River. At this base his men worked at building boats to carry crews and equipment down the Tanana when the ice broke.

The men had only crude tools, but they built fine boats. Five were quite large, some eighteen feet in length. Each would hold a ton of cargo, four oarsmen, and a steersman. For Mitchell's personal use there was a smaller boat about twelve feet long.

The boats were used to carry the working parties

down the river along the route of the line to be built. The men in these parties erected the poles, installed the insulators, and tied on the telegraph wire. Taking Dutch De Haus with him, Mitchell went ahead of the workers to determine the course of the line.

When he found a suitable place to land, he would go ashore and with his compass lay a straight line from one point to another. Then, working alone, he blazed a trail through. He could lay out from five to ten miles a day in this way.

"It was difficult," he reported, "working through the underbrush, bogs and wet moss, but much easier and quicker than carrying a big outfit and several men along."

Mitchell found great satisfaction in testing himself against the wilderness.

As the party reached the point where there was only a hundred miles more to go to finish the line, the lieutenant embarked on one of the most hazardous journeys of his career. He decided to take one of the larger boats, containing food supplies, and handle it himself. He wanted to be sure that nothing happened to it on the way down.

His friend Dutch and three other men went with him. All were manning the oars, while Mitchell stood in the stern and steered the boat by means of a twenty-foot oar called a sweep.

The river had widened and the water had become much swifter. The strong current carried along sizable trees, which in some places lodged on the bends or sandbars. They formed great heaps like log jams, with the current roaring beneath them. The river channels were crooked. Green trees growing out from the banks hung over the river, sweeping up and down in the water. Mitchell's task as steersman was to avoid both these and the tremendous piles of driftwood.

It was not easy, but the boat made very good time and the pilot was able to avoid the dangers that loomed on every side. Suddenly, however, the channel narrowed. The current grew even swifter. Looking ahead, Mitchell saw a sharp turn around which the water swirled viciously. Hanging out over the river at this point was a long spruce tree, which whipped in and out of the water.

Mitchell saw the danger. He thought of it in terms of his job. If the tree hit the boat they would surely be swamped and lose their food supply. That would delay the work another year.

"Put on speed!" he shouted to his men as the boat shot for the point.

His plan was to bring the boat toward the eddy at

the bend. He hoped the darting water would carry it to safety. As the boat neared the point, he pulled his steering sweep with all his strength.

But it was no use. The swinging tree swooped down and caught him across the waist. An instant later the tree had swung upward, carrying Mitchell with it. He held onto the tree for dear life.

Below him was a big pile of driftwood with the water gushing beneath it. Mitchell knew that if he let go of the tree he would be swept under the driftwood. That would be the end of him.

As these thoughts flashed through his mind the tree to which he clung dipped him into the icy water and swung again into the air. Up and down it went.

"Hold on!" Dutch yelled.

Mitchell could hear the other men shouting as they headed for the shore. He saw the boat brought to land a quarter of a mile downriver.

He had wrapped both his arms and legs around the swinging tree. He found that he could hold his breath for the space of time he was ducked into the river. Perhaps he could hang on for fifteen or twenty minutes. No longer, he knew.

Three men leaped from the boat the instant it touched the shore. The fourth lingered only long enough to make the boat fast to a tree on the bank.

Then, carrying with them a coil of rope, all the men rushed upstream to the bend. Three of them tied the rope around Dutch, over his right shoulder and under his left arm, then made a final turn around his body. They wrapped the other end of the rope around a tree.

Watching from his dangerous perch, Mitchell saw his friend leap into the river. The rope was let out gradually by the other men until Dutch reached the point where the swinging tree was flashing up and down. As Mitchell emerged from his last ducking, Dutch grabbed him around both shoulders. They held onto each other with a viselike grip. The three men on shore pulled them in.

As the drenched, shivering pair stepped on solid land once more, Dutch turned to Mitchell with a grin.

"I don't know if we are even," he said, "but you saved me from freezing last winter, and I have pulled you out of a bad place in this river."

Mitchell considered that they were more than "even." He never forgot Dutch De Haus, the man who saved his life.

There was no further trouble as they completed the last twenty miles of the trip down the river. For two weeks after that, Mitchell's men, fully experienced now and caught up by his enthusiasm, worked with great speed as they chopped through the right-of-way to meet another group that was working toward them.

It was late June. Mitchell was confident now that the job would be completed that summer. He felt a great sense of satisfaction as he personally made the last connection of the Alaska telegraph system. That was on June 27, 1903.

"Then," Mitchell reported with triumph and pride, "from St. Michael and Nome on the Bering Sea, clear through to New York and Washington, the electric current transmitted our messages with the speed of light. Alaska was at last open to civilization. No longer was it the land of the unknown, sealed tight by the God of Everlasting Snow and Frost. We had forced open the portals with which he shut out the white man from the North."

The first telegraph message to come from the interior of Alaska over entirely American wire was addressed to General A. W. Greely, head of the Army Signal Corps. Consisting of just seven words, it read: "REPORT LINE THROUGH ALASKA COMPLETED. WILLIAM MITCHELL."

CHAPTER FIVE

On December 17, 1903, not long after Mitchell's return to the United States from Alaska, two brothers named Wilbur and Orville Wright made man's first flight in a motor-driven airplane. This feat, which was to prove so important to the world and to Billy Mitchell personally, attracted little attention.

Mitchell himself probably did not know about the flight at the time. He was on his honeymoon.

It was not a sudden marriage. Before going to Alaska he had become engaged to a childhood friend, Caroline Stoddard, who lived in Rochester, New York. Her mother and Billy's mother were girlhood friends. When they were in school together they had talked of how nice it would be if, in later years, one had a son and the other a daughter so they could marry each other. And it turned out that way.

Caroline and Billy were married on December 2, 1903. The young bridegroom took his wife on a honeymoon trip to Cuba and Mexico.

Typically, he conducted an investigation of United States military defenses in the Caribbean even though he was on his honeymoon. He studied the history of Mexico, telling his bride where armies were stationed at different times in the past.

Billy Mitchell now instinctively thought and acted the part of a military man—although not then or ever one of the hidebound variety. Shortly before his return from Alaska he was still uncertain about his life's work. He wrote his father about the possibility of going into business, but added, "Of course, I am naturally a sort of soldier. I like the service, I like to have my command, and I like service in the field, and don't like to live in crowded cities."

His doubts about his career had been settled. He was an officer of the United States Army and would remain one. He was a captain, too, having been promoted from first lieutenant. At twenty-four, he was the youngest captain in the army.

Mitchell settled down to the relatively quiet life of a regular army officer in peacetime. He devoted most of his spare time to study and scientific experiments involving the work of the Signal Corps. He became interested in the part airborne craft, particularly balloons, could play in military observation.

In May, 1904, while stationed in Colorado, he wrote his father: "I have made a few drawings of new instruments and appliances which I shall forward to the Signal Office during the coming week.

Captain Mitchell in full-dress uniform.

This and some investigations in balloon work have been my week's work."

He was fascinated with the possibilities of aerial observation. In army maneuvers held that year in Virginia, with the forces divided into two groups for training, Mitchell made practical application of one of his ideas.

He picked out the highest hill in the area and on top of it erected a 200-foot tower. The day the maneuvers began, he climbed up the tower and with field glasses could clearly see the "enemy" forces as they concentrated in preparation for battle. He was able to identify the different units and turn the information over to his army commander.

Under the rules of the war game, this meant defeat for the other side. Since no one but Mitchell had received any training up to this point, the war was declared over and a new one was started. This time Captain Mitchell and his high tower were ruled unfair.

His busy mind was constantly at work to devise new methods and to improve old methods of carrying out the Signal Corps' mission. He was responsible for the adoption by the army of a system of controlling artillery firing by telephone communications. He pioneered in military photography. He worked out a plan of taking pictures from kites and having them developed for use within an hour.

Mitchell visited the St. Louis Exposition in 1904. On exhibit there was a small, engine-powered dirigible developed by Thomas Scott Baldwin, an early bird of aviation. The year after Mitchell's visit to the Exposition, the Signal Corps bought from Baldwin the first dirigible for the army.

His trip to St. Louis afforded a wonderful example of the mutual trust and confidence that always existed between Mitchell and men under his command. He was in charge of a company of men on their way from Washington to Fort Leavenworth, Kansas. He asked his superior officer to be permitted to stop in St. Louis so his men could see the Exposition.

No, he was told, that would not be allowed as

Captain Mitchell and Signal Corps troops.

his men would be certain to misbehave.

Mitchell retorted that he would be personally responsible for their good behavior. Furthermore, he added, he would himself pay their expenses at the big show.

Permission was granted on these terms. Mitchell was not in the least surprised when, after enjoying the Exposition to the fullest, the company showed up to a man at the railroad station the next day at the hour that had been set. All were sober and fit for duty, just as their captain had foreseen.

This was the only organized Signal Corps company in the army, and at times duty called it far afield. Such a time came in April 1906 when the California city of San Francisco was struck by an earthquake, followed by a disastrous fire. Much of the city lay in ruins. Disorder broke out in the streets. Mitchell and his men received orders to report immediately to San Francisco.

When the company arrived there, Mitchell found that General Funston, his old friend of the Philippines, was in charge. He had occupied the stricken city with troops.

General Greely, in command of the Pacific Division, with headquarters at San Francisco, was out of the city when the disaster occurred. He rushed back at once, and he and Funston set to work to organize the relief of the thousands of stricken people.

Mitchell's job was to restore the lines of transportation and communication, all of which had either been destroyed or put temporarily out of service. Not even a direct telegraph line to San Francisco was available. The water system was not functioning. Many thousands of people were homeless, and food was in short supply. The city was still in flames.

"Houses were being blown up to stop the spread of the fire," Mitchell wrote later. "The streets in the lower part of the city were a terrible mass of wreckage, through which a way had to be blown with dynamite. Hundreds of people were dead, the exact number will never be known. More than 200,000 were homeless and without food."

Under military command the badly damaged city was divided into six districts. Mitchell was placed in charge of the largest district. Soldiers patrolled the streets to prevent looters from helping themselves to goods from the shops.

The plight of San Francisco had aroused the sympathy of the whole country. Food and clothing poured into the city. The army distributed this among the needy citizens, established soup kitchens, and built shelters for the homeless.

San Francisco after the earthquake, showing the beginning of rebuilding amid the destruction.

Mitchell was proud of the way his men performed to bring order out of chaos.

"It was a revelation to me," he said afterward, "to see men who were masters of business and captains of industry utterly at a loss and incapable of any initiative in such a terrible emergency. And it was equally interesting to see how the officers of the military service, from second lieutenant up, who were trained to act definitely and quickly in emergencies, did exactly the right thing under the most trying and difficult circumstances."

However, he paid tribute to the bravery of the people of San Francisco in the face of the disaster.

The city's leaders already were making plans to re-build the ruined city. Billy Mitchell had a deeply rooted respect for that kind of enterprise.

After his duty in San Francisco, Mitchell was kept on the move by the army. He was stationed at various military posts in the United States. In the fall of 1906, when this country was trying to bolster up the weak republican government in Cuba, Mitchell went again to that island as chief signal officer. He did a remarkable job of reorganizing and rebuilding Cuba's telegraph system in less than a year.

He also went again to the Philippines, this time to serve as chief signal officer for the Department of Luzon. He took advantage of his stay there to make an investigation of Japan's ventures into the area. He found that the Japanese had established wireless stations on small islands near the Philippines. He reported this to the War Department, then took leave to go to Japan and study that country's military system.

One observation he made on this trip was that Japan was already building an air force. At the end of 1911 it consisted of only twelve planes, but even this small number placed it far ahead of the United States.

This was a matter of much interest to Mitchell.

He had met Orville Wright a few years before. The meeting was the beginning of a long friendship. He was impressed with Wright's ideas about the military importance of the airplane.

Mitchell could see that this new flying machine could make it much easier for the Signal Corps to observe enemy movements, which was part of its assigned mission. Balloons already were being used for this work, but the airplane—if it should be made to work—would give much greater flexibility to the operation. Mitchell's imagination was fired as he considered the possibilities.

He took his growing interest in airplanes with him to a new assignment in 1912. He was ordered to Washington to serve on the general staff of the army. At the age of thirty-two, he was the youngest officer ever to be assigned to such service.

He had the important duty of receiving and analyzing all military information coming to the War Department from Europe. The Balkan Wars had broken out. They were a prelude to World War I, which was to make Mitchell a world renowned leader in military aviation.

CHAPTER SIX

IN THOSE EARLY DAYS of aviation, flying was an individual adventure. Airplane pilots were few in number and were generally reckoned to be a reckless breed. They took to the air with a minimum of training. Such training as they had was of a most informal nature. There were no full-time pilots, as flying was indulged in only by those who could afford it and were not afraid. Flying was a sport, not a vocation.

The planes were rickety and of uncertain performance. There were no flying fields as such. Most takeoffs and landings were made in country pastures, and the pilots had to keep a sharp lookout for farm animals.

Military aviation hardly existed in the United States. In 1909 the army had bought one plane from

Orville Wright. The aviation section of the Signal Corps was made up of three pilots and ten enlisted men. In that year Russia already had seventy-nine officers and 3,255 enlisted men engaged in military flying. France, England, and Germany had aviation forces almost as large.

At the time Billy Mitchell began his assignment on the general staff of the army, the United States was still at the bottom of the list of world powers in air strength. As late as the middle of 1913, only seven officers in the Signal Corps held military aviators' licenses.

It was at about this time that Mitchell testified before the Military Affairs Committee of the House of Representatives on a proposal to create a separate aviation corps. He thought the time had not come for that. Some bombs had been dropped from airplanes in the Balkan Wars, but Mitchell said the principal role of military aviation was still to conduct observation and reconnaissance missions.

The value of the airplane as an offensive weapon against an enemy was still in an experimental stage, he declared.

Mitchell also told the congressional committee that centralized control was necessary to develop military aviation adequately. "We have all of a sudden awakened to the knowledge that we are behind all other countries in the matter of aviation," he pointed out.

He urged the importance of naming a permanent directing head in Washington to promote aviation. He suggested that officers be encouraged to take up flying by offers of rapid promotion for doing so.

Enthusiastic as he was about aviation, Mitchell had never piloted a plane. In the winter of 1915, when he was thirty-six years of age, he decided to do something about this.

He enrolled in the flying school conducted at Newport News, Virginia, by the Curtiss Company, one of the country's few manufacturers of airplanes. He not only had to take the lessons on his own time but also had to pay for them himself.

"The only time I could get away was on Sunday," he said of this experience. "I used to take a boat down the Potomac River from Washington to Newport News on Saturday night, fly all day Sunday, and be back in the office on Monday."

After four Sundays of flying instruction, he was sent aloft on his first solo flight. As long as he was in the air he did well enough, but on coming down he made a bad landing. The plane was cracked up, although not badly. Mitchell was not injured.

He regarded the accident as a fortunate event, "which taught me more than anything that ever happened to me in the air." Mitchell was always adventurous and might even at times be considered flamboyant, but he was not reckless.

General war had started in Europe in August of 1914. There was much talk that the United States would remain sternly neutral. Mitchell was among those who were convinced that sooner or later this country would be involved in the war. And he knew the United States was not prepared.

In the field of his special interest, military aviation, he noted that at the outbreak of the war the U.S. "air force" consisted of just fourteen planes. Every major European country had an air force of several hundred planes. Out of 2,400 persons qualified as fliers in the whole world, the United States had only fifty.

Billy Mitchell, now promoted to major, wrote a report on "Our Faulty Military Policy" for the Army War College in July, 1915. Questions of military policy had been neglected, he stated, because the American people thought the country was safe from aggression. Mitchell disagreed with this theory.

"Without preparation in time of peace," he wrote in his report, "no nation today has the remotest chance of defending itself against a world power.

"The military policy of the United States," he continued, "is and has been to prepare for war *after such war has actually broken out,* and to have practically no machinery in time of peace with which an army could be created with rapidity."

Mitchell was absolutely certain that it was only a matter of time until the United States would enter the war on the side of the Allied Powers. He wanted his country to be ready to meet the fearsome responsibility.

When he was appointed head of the aviation section, he threw himself with energy and enthusiasm into the task of enlarging the tiny air force.

He met with instant opposition. The War Department was dominated by senior officers who were in the habit of thinking in terms of the last war instead of the next one. They believed in horse soldiers and foot soldiers; they did not believe in flying machines. Some of them looked on Mitchell as a young upstart who wanted to change everything.

Nevertheless, the newly named chief of the army's aviation section, working with some officers who were friendly and with interested civilians, was successful in getting a substantial appropriation from Congress. President Woodrow Wilson authorized the establishment of an aviation reserve corps of 500 fliers. However, the army had no facilities for training would-be military aviators. There was another obstacle to be overcome.

Mitchell turned to the private aviation schools for help. He made agreements with a number of them to train pilots, with the government paying the cost. Then he launched a nationwide campaign to enroll students for these training courses.

In the closing months of 1916 and the early part of 1917, the war in Europe had reached a critical stage for the Allies. The great naval fleet of England was under constant attack by German submarines. The French army suffered a severe defeat. Revolution had broken out in Russia, and the Russian armies could no longer be depended upon to press the German forces from their rear. Germany was showing greater strength week by week.

Mitchell, observing all this, saw that progress on the ground by the armies in Europe had almost halted. Neither side was able to advance or retreat. Air operations, on the other hand, were constantly increasing in importance and effectiveness. If the war lasted another two or three years, he told other officers in the War Department, air power would be the deciding element.

He wanted to get off to Europe and see for himself what was going on. Spain was not in the war, and on March 17, 1917, Mitchell left Washington to go to that country as an official military observer on aviation.

He found Spain, as he reported, "in rather a nervous state." The country was crowded with spies from all countries. Newspapers were filled with propaganda put out by agents of every nation involved in the war. Mitchell was spied upon wherever he went.

He talked with a Spanish officer who had recently returned from a visit to the German army. He found the Spaniard distant and suspicious. Obviously, he thought Mitchell's country would soon be in the war against Germany, the belligerent generally favored in Spain.

Although the Spanish army as a whole sympathized with the Germans, Mitchell doubted that Spain would enter the war. Even if it did, he concluded, the military value of its entrance would not be high.

He was still in Spain on April 6 when the United States Congress passed a declaration of war against Germany. He set out at once to cross the border into war-torn France.

Captain Mitchell took this photo of a Spanish Zeppelin detecting device.

"The change was astounding," he wrote. "The people looked tired, strained, haggard; no young men were to be seen on the streets. The guards consisted of men over forty years of age. Few horses and mules were to be seen, as all serviceable animals had been sent north to the armies."

Mitchell reached Paris on April 10. He found deep gloom on all sides. Plans had been made for a spring offensive, with the British and French armies attacking the Germans from two sides at the same time. But the Germans, foreseeing such a plan, had retired from the front of the British army. As they withdrew, they destroyed everything that lay in their path: towns, factories, roads, farms, forests. They blew up bridges and dammed rivers and canals in order to flood the countryside.

This left the British unable to advance for at least two months. They could not cross the devastated area with heavy guns, ammunition, and supplies in time to attack the Germans before spring was over.

"What a foolish kind of war this seemed," Mitchell exclaimed, "where an army could not advance twenty or thirty miles for months, even with nobody opposing them! How could such an army ever possibly end a war, except by direct pressure? It seemed to me that the utility of ground armies was rapidly falling to about zero, due to the great defense power of modern firearms."

In Paris, he reported to the American Ambassador and immediately started setting up an office to handle aviation matters. He had no funds from Washington and had no Americans to man his office.

He borrowed two officers from the French army and, after consulting with the French Aeronautic Headquarters, began preparing a plan for the hoped-for American aviation setup. A list was made of all necessary equipment, showing the kinds of airplanes, types of engines and instruments, and an estimate of the raw materials that would be required.

Ten days after Mitchell's arrival in Paris, the

complete program that he thought was needed had been written out and sent to Washington.

Having accomplished this, he applied for and received permission to join the French army at the front. He knew that months would elapse before the force of the United States could make itself fully felt in the war. Meanwhile, he was determined to learn at firsthand all that he could about what needed to be done.

He set out by train for the town of Châlons, close to where the fighting was going on. Within a few days he was to become the first American officer to serve with the Allies under German fire.

CHAPTER SEVEN

BILLY MITCHELL REMEMBERED with a smile the five-year-old boy who had vowed that he would never again speak French. Now the grown-up military officer found himself talking every day with Frenchmen in their own language. His knowledge of French came back quickly.

The people in the hotel at Châlons where he took living quarters did not know at first what to make of this smiling, affable, hard-working American. Late at night they could hear the clicking of his typewriter as he wrote his notes and recommendations. They did not understand. Finally, Mitchell learned, they came to the conclusion that he was operating some kind of strange radio telegraph instrument.

One of the women at the hotel mentioned this

to Mitchell. He cleared up the mystery by showing her the typewriter and reading her something he had written on it. She passed the word on to others in the hotel. Most of them had never seen an American before.

"Many of the people really expected to see us with feathers in our hair," Mitchell said, "like the pictures of American Indians in their books."

He did not spend much of his time in the hotel. He was eager to get to the front. Equipped with helmet, gas mask, and field glasses, he asked a French officer, Captain Raulin, to take him to a place where an attack was going on.

"It is too dangerous," the Frenchmen protested. "If an American officer should be killed just now it would have a very bad effect in your country."

"Our country is at war the same as yours," Mitchell replied. "We are allies. I need to find out what is necessary in this kind of warfare."

"*Eh bien*," said Captain Raulin. "You are the judge."

Off to the western front they went. The opposing armies faced each other across no-man's-land from trenches they had dug out of the earth. The Germans had been in occupation of French territory for almost three years. War had laid waste the countryside.

The French soldiers were worn out and dispirited.

Many of them came out of their trenches to view the strange sight of an American among them. Mitchell talked to the men and their officers, inspected the dugouts, visited first aid stations. Everything was placed underground for protection against artillery fire.

One day the American was with the French foot soldiers in the trenches as they launched an attack. He was later decorated by the French government for his action at the front.

Mitchell made a thorough study of the methods used by the French in their aerial bombing. He noted that the bombardment people "are sure that if they are given enough planes and explosives there would be nothing left of Germany in a short while." For his part, he was more than ever convinced that the war could be won only through air power.

"A very significant thing to me," he reported, "was that we could cross the lines of these contending armies in a few minutes in our airplane, whereas the armies have been locked in the struggle, immovable, powerless to advance for three years. The whole area over which the Germans and French have battled is not more than sixty miles across. They get nowhere as far as ending the war is concerned."

Billy Mitchell (extreme right) with friends on a French battlefield.

Mitchell was out in the field, often under fire, for ten days. Every night he returned to his hotel and busied himself at his typewriter, setting down what he had seen and information he had gathered.

He visited the aviation bombardment squadrons, which were stationed at what in peacetime had been one of France's largest school for fliers. He attended some classes in a course given officers and balloon observation companies. He even went up in a balloon and from the air watched a battle below.

France, he noted, was far ahead of the United States in every phase of aviation. Even so, the Germans had by this time almost swept the Allies from the sky. French aviation was on the defensive in most areas and was barely holding its own in others. He pointed this out in one of his frequent reports to the War Department.

"The men have been at this too long and have lost their nerve, with very few exceptions," he stated bluntly. "If we feed in our own organization by driblets, our men will have the nerve taken out of them also. We must keep our whole organization separate, under our own command, and go in and clean up the air. The function of pursuit squadrons is to take and maintain the offensive, to seek the enemy and attack him wherever found, and to destroy him. After three years of fighting, the French are no longer able to do this. They have no more nerve left in the majority of their pilots."

Again and again, Mitchell sent urgent word to Washington that airplane manufacture must be greatly expanded and speeded up. Many additional pilots must be trained. The air service must be made at least five times stronger in men and material.

In May he visited the British army. General Hugh Trenchard was in command of the Royal Air Force. His headquarters were at Abbeville, about twenty miles from the front. Mitchell noticed that the English soldiers appeared to be in much better shape than the French, who had borne the brunt of the first three years of the war.

Mitchell liked General Trenchard on sight. There was something about him that inspired confidence. A tall man who held himself very straight, he was decided in manner and direct in speech.

Trenchard was a pilot himself. Mitchell knew that he was really the father of British military aviation. Under his leadership, the Royal Air Force had grown from a few second-class planes to a great fighting force with more than 2,000 aircraft on the line.

Trenchard welcomed Mitchell and, without wasting any time, asked him what he wanted to know.

Mitchell matched the senior officer's directness.

"I want to learn all about your organization, your equipment, and your supply system," he said. "Also, I'd like to participate with your aircraft in any operations that are now taking place against the Germans."

The other man was somewhat taken aback. "That's quite an order," he observed. "And just how much time do you propose to give to this?"

"Why, I think the first part could be gone over this afternoon and evening," Mitchell replied with assurance. "Then we can start the next part tomorrow morning."

"Do you think, Major, that I have no other duty than to show you around and tell you everything you want to know?"

The general's words were crisp, but there was a twinkle in his British eyes.

"General Trenchard, I know you have such an excellent organization that it will run itself without your leadership for a day or two."

"All right," Trenchard said, laughing, "I guess you'll get what you want."

The two men got along famously. Trenchard took his visitor on a fast but complete tour of inspection. Mitchell found to his delight that the general was not a man bound by military tradition.

"The great captains," said General Trenchard, "are those who think out new methods and then put them into execution. Anybody can always use the old methods."

While he was in the area, Mitchell was flown over the British front. He could see fighting going on in the trenches below.

Mitchell spent four days with the British army. Never, he said, had he learned so much in such a short time.

"Nor," he added with enthusiasm, "have I ever met a man with whom it was a greater pleasure to talk than General Trenchard."

Back at his own headquarters, he found his little office in excellent shape. The necessary information to move ahead had been obtained and plans of organization written out. The U.S. air force in France consisted of exactly one plane, a Nieuport which Mitchell used himself.

However, several hundred Americans were being trained in French aviation schools. Mitchell made arrangements with the country's minister of aviation to equip them with French planes. Within a month or two, he planned, five or six American squadrons would be ready to fight the Germans.

General John J. Pershing had been named commander of the American Expeditionary Force in Europe. He came to Paris in June and brought with him Major Townsend F. Dodd, his aviation officer.

Dodd told Mitchell, who was now a lieutenant colonel and the highest ranking American aviation officer in Europe, about the great effort being made to train military fliers in the United States. He thought some would be coming over within a few months. But Dodd expressed doubt that many efficient planes could be sent over in less than a year.

Mitchell took a flight every day, accompanied by Adjutant Fumat, his instructor. One day while aloft they encountered a terrific storm. Rain poured around them in torrents. As they looked down from their plane, they could see trees being toppled by the wind.

The light plane could not fly against the wind, so they decided they must land. Fumat headed the airplane down toward a wheat field. As it neared the ground, Mitchell saw an old man and woman driving along in a cart, "holding up their hands as though in supplication to the Almighty that we be saved."

A crash seemed inevitable. The plane went down toward the wheat field, reeling in the gale. Just as it touched the ground, a horde of French soldiers came rushing out of a house at one end of the field. They surrounded the plane, shouting to one another, and caught hold of its wings. The little craft was brought to an almost immediate stop and no damage was done.

The commanding officer of the troops invited the two rain-soaked aviators into the house until the storm was over. He gave them a good meal and warm drinks while their clothing dried.

An hour later they took off from a road running through the field. Soon they landed safely at Le Bourget airdrome, which they had left only a little while before.

The next day they were up in the air again.

From left to right: Sergeant Fumat, Lt. Col. Mitchell, Major Harmon, Baron Desturnelle at Le Bourget Airdrome, July 1917.

Mitchell and Fumat flew all over northern France.

"This not only gave me wonderful practice in flying," Mitchell rejoiced, "but also a splendid knowledge of the country. No one in the ground army had this advantage of getting over the country so much, and consequently none knew it as well as I."

The great wave of American soldiers was still to come. But some troops from the United States already were to be seen in the streets of Paris. General Pershing and his staff established their headquarters in the city.

Considerable pressure was being applied to get the commander-in-chief to approve placing the Americans into French and English regiments as individuals rather than as organizations. One day Pershing asked Mitchell what he thought of this proposal.

"Why, General, so far as I'm concerned, I will serve in an American army or nothing," Mitchell replied.

Pershing was known as a rather stern, unbending man. He now fixed the younger officer with a serious gaze, his gray mustache bristling.

"What do you mean by that?" he demanded.

"We came over here to fight as Americans," Mitchell declared. "We are fighting our own war. At the end of the war we may find we need our own army as badly as we needed it during the war. If we fail to develop an army and fighting methods, we may come out of the war as dependents of European nations."

Pershing indulged in a rare smile and said nothing more. Mitchell knew the general felt the same way, and that he was having some difficulty in convincing Washington officials that this was the correct attitude.

But this was the course followed throughout the war. The American military units maintained their own identities, fighting as parts of the American Expeditionary Force. Pershing was rigid in discipline, but he always stood up for his own men.

Mitchell held his commanding general in deep respect. He only wished Pershing would—or could—

move faster in matters having to do with aviation. Still, he realized that the general had problems of his own. Among them was the fact that some officers back in the United States were anxious to take his place as commander-in-chief. Also, some of those officers still doubted the value of aviation in military operations.

In August the news reached Paris that Congress had passed laws creating a large aviation corps. It was to consist of 10,000 officers and 90,000 enlisted men. Millions of dollars had been appropriated for planes and material.

Unfortunately, as Mitchell soon learned, his recommendation as to what planes should be used had been ignored. He had recommended "the fine and suitable French airplanes." A plane of English design had been adopted instead. It was obsolete and dangerous, Mitchell declared, "a flaming coffin" for his pilots. Besides, he said, the engine the Americans intended for use in the British design was unsuited to the plane. He did not understand why his recommendation had not been followed.

More than ever, Mitchell wanted to get out of Paris and closer to the front. In Paris, he said, "most of the fighting was done around restaurant tables and in political committee rooms."

This did not suit him at all. He wanted to be

where the fighting squadrons were in action.

He soon realized his desire. The high command decided to separate control of the Air Service in the United States from the air forces in the war area. Mitchell was named commander of the latter.

The French armies were beginning an attack in the area around the city of Verdun. Mitchell promptly went there, acting as observer as a French pilot flew him over the front. He noted that both sides in the fighting had more planes in the air than when he had been there a few weeks before.

"I saw two aerial combats, both at a short distance," he wrote later. "In the first one, the French plane went down in flames, shooting to the earth with a long trail of very black smoke, caused by the ignition of the gasoline. This was a terrible sight.

"We in the air feared being burned alive more than anything else. There was nothing we could do, as none of the planes were equipped with parachutes. They had not yet been applied to use on the front except by the balloonists; but we could just as well have had them on airplanes and many a good man would have been saved."

As the summer of 1917 drew to a close, Mitchell established living quarters for himself and his staff in a large house near Chaumont. He wanted his principal officers close around him so that they would always be available to him and to one another. Their office headquarters were set up in an old French barracks not far from the house.

Mitchell had assembled an excellent group of officers on his staff. He put them to studying French and encouraged them to talk in that language as much as possible. Arrangements were completed for placing the aviation troops on the line of battle.

Serious business lay ahead. Mitchell was determined that his men should be ready for it.

CHAPTER EIGHT

ON A COLD, WET OCTOBER morning a French pilot took Mitchell aloft in a light plane so he could observe a battle being waged on the ground. After they had been in the air for about two hours, Mitchell could see that the pilot was getting very tired. He signaled him to return to the landing field.

As the plane approached the field, Mitchell noted that the wind had changed direction about ninety degrees since their takeoff. But, to his mounting alarm, the pilot was landing just as if the wind had not changed. The plane came in fast with the wind blowing straight against its side.

The pilot set the wheels down hard. The plane bounced twenty feet into the air. Landing again, it hit a muddy place and flipped over.

Although the plane was smashed to pieces, Mitchell was not hurt. He quickly got out of his observer's seat and looked into the forward cockpit. He saw that the pilot was jammed helplessly into his seat. Mitchell, the fear of fire uppermost in his mind, quickly pulled the Frenchman out of the wrecked plane.

"The plane did not catch fire and neither of us was hurt to amount to anything," Mitchell related, "but the pilot felt terribly about it. He had once taken the Queen of the Belgians up on a flight and now he had crashed with the commander of the American Air Service."

Mitchell excused the pilot because he knew he was exhausted. "Few people can appreciate how very tired an airman gets in action," he said.

All the same, he made up his mind that this was the last time any pilot would fly him during the war unless he was incapacitated for piloting his own plane.

He knew that flying in wartime was not a safe occupation, but he saw no reason to court danger unnecessarily. There were enough unavoidable risks.

That winter of 1917-18 was the coldest France had known in many years. The airplanes had water-cooled engines, and a great problem was to keep them from freezing. Water had to be heated in great pots before being poured into the plane. Pilots and observers flying at high altitudes often had their noses frozen.

Remembering the rabbit fur protector he had created for his nose in Alaska, Mitchell ordered some aviation suits made up of waterproof gaberdine and lined with thick Belgian hare fur. He also bought a fine flying cap made of mink inside and out. On his feet he wore sheepskin moccasins with the wool turned inward.

All through the winter, preparations went forward for an intensive drive against the enemy when spring came. The Americans established special

Billy Mitchell in winter flying suit at the front in France.

schools for pursuit, observation, and bombardment aviation.

Things were beginning to work smoothly, but Mitchell was dismayed when the first shipload of aviation officers arrived in France.

Almost none of them, he declared, had ever even seen an airplane. In fact, he added, "A more incompetent lot of air warriors had never arrived in the zone of active military operation since the war began."

Most of the staff officers were non-fliers, and Mitchell noted darkly that they tried to rid the staff of actual fliers who had superior rank.

This was the reason, he surmised, that he was assigned to command the Air Service of the First Army Headquarters, which had headquarters at a town called Neufchâteau near the front. The non-fliers wanted him out of the way. However, the assignment suited him because all the troops of the line were to be assigned to this corps and he would have the opportunity of training them. Also he liked the First Army commander, General Hunter Liggett and considered him one of the ablest soldiers he knew.

As spring came on, the war grew hotter. German cannons fired into Paris. Constant airplane raids also were made on the city. Many citizens left the capital and fled into the countryside.

Mitchell was hard at work on battle training for the fliers assigned to his command. He found that they were wonderful pilots so far as flying went, but he was concerned about how they would perform in actual combat with the enemy. He comforted himself with the knowledge that with every day of training his men showed up to better advantage.

The fliers were young and high-spirited. After the day's training was over they looked for fun. When an American hospital unit with a number of pretty nurses moved into a nearby French hospital, Mitchell's pilots were overjoyed. Soon they were going off to visit the nurses whenever they could get an evening free.

After a time the commanding officer of the hospital unit complained to Mitchell that the fliers were keeping the nurses up too late, making the young women "good for nothing" the next day. Mitchell, amused, issued instructions that the gentleman callers were to come home earlier.

Most of the men obeyed, but a few did not. The hospital commander therefore gave orders that none of the nurses should go out with the pilots or see them at any time.

He came the next day to report to Mitchell with considerable irritation what happened next. That

morning, he said, several of the American planes had
flown in formation over the hospital and bombarded
it with rolls of toilet paper. The long streamers of
paper covered the tops of the buildings and hung,
waving in the wind, from telegraph wires. The hospital officer wanted the fliers severely disciplined.

Mitchell went to the hospital to see for himself.
It was, he said, the funniest sight he had seen in a long
time. He concealed his mirth from the other officers,
but took no disciplinary action except to tell his men
to "cut out all foolishness" in the future.

They had less time for "foolishness." By the end
of April, Mitchell's men were in full action on the
front and were acquitting themselves well.

Their commanding officer himself flew over the
lines almost every day to keep track of every squadron in his organization. As he flew on his observation
missions, he wished he could be one of the squadron
pilots.

"During the Spanish-American War," he recalled
wistfully, "when I joined the First Wisconsin Infantry
as a private, I had more fun than any other time."

His duties now were far different. When he was
not flying he was likely to be fighting with higher
headquarters on behalf of his men. It seemed a great
shame to him that practically no high-ranking officer

on the general staff was an experienced pilot.

"The general staff," he said bluntly, "was trying to run the Air Service with just as much knowledge about it as a hog has about skating."

Being Billy Mitchell, he did not hesitate to speak his mind. He had many discussions with General Pershing on the subject. Sometimes the talks became heated arguments, with both men raising their voices and pounding the table with their fists.

On one such occasion, General Pershing said sternly, "Colonel Mitchell, if you do not stop insisting that the organization of the Air Force be changed, I will send you back to the United States."

Mitchell stared at him. "If you do," he shot back, "you could soon come after me!"

Pershing returned his gaze, then unexpectedly laughed. The talk ended amicably.

The American fliers were coming to be regarded as saviors by the French people. One day in May, the alarm that a German plane was approaching sounded in a little village only six miles from Mitchell's headquarters. The village people ran for their cellars.

Then they heard the roar of an American plane as it headed toward the enemy.

"The Americans are coming!" the people shouted to one another. "We will be saved."

Coming out of their cellars, the villagers stared in fascinated horror as the two airplanes came close together, their pilots firing at each other. As they drew apart, the American plane turned upside down. The pilot tumbled out, apparently in his haste having failed to fasten his seat belt. His plane caught fire and crashed to the ground.

The German plane withdrew, but later was forced by French planes to land. The pilot and his observer were captured.

The death of the American pilot, Major Raoul Lufbery, was a severe blow to Mitchell. Lufbery had been his personal friend as well as the unit's leading pilot.

Another great loss was suffered by Mitchell only a few days later when his younger brother was killed in an airplane crash at an air depot in France. It seemed to him, the older man said, that if either of them had to be killed he should have been the one. His brother was only twenty-three years old.

The deaths of these two men, coming so close together, spurred the pilots in Mitchell's group to renewed efforts against the enemy. As for their commanding officer, on the afternoon of his brother's military funeral, he flew over the front to inspect all the aircraft and pilots on duty there.

This was an everyday activity for Mitchell. He flew alone and without a protective escort. Other planes accompanying him would have slowed him down and caused the movement to be more easily observed by enemy fliers.

He had assigned to his unit the fastest airplanes on the western front. Typically, he had also acquired the fastest automobile in France. He was a familiar figure, and a dashing one, as he traveled all over the country by air and by land.

The men in the Air Service of the First Army almost idolized their commander. He was, they agreed, "the snappiest officer in the service." In addition, they knew he worked harder and put in longer hours than anyone in his command. They boasted that he would never ask his men to do anything which

General Mitchell and his driver in France.

he would not undertake himself.

This was the man who was preparing to lead the greatest combat offensive by air the world had ever known.

On the ground, the Germans had thrown their last desperate strength into an all-out attack on the western front. They made great advances, destroying French units which tried to stand against them. French airfields and the planes on them were captured.

"The flower of German aviation is concentrated over their victorious army," Mitchell reported in July. "Now is the time to get into it whether we are ready or not."

The American forces were fast getting ready.

The greatest army the United States had ever put into the field was being assembled in France in that summer of 1918. The troop ships plied across the Atlantic, bringing thousands upon thousands of khaki-clad soldiers. The Americans filled the roads of France. Almost everything on wheels in the country was called into service to bring up supplies for them.

Mitchell begged for airplanes, more planes and more planes. He was determined to assemble an air force strong enough to keep the war planes of Germany from demoralizing American ground troops in the great battle he knew was coming.

By the end of August he had under his command a force of 1,476 airplanes and 20 balloons. Thirty thousand officers and men handled the planes. They were stationed at fourteen main flying fields and a great many substations. This was by far the greatest concentration of air power that had ever been known.

The force included French, British and Italian as well as American units. Mitchell rejoiced that the fliers from four nations were here "acting together with no discord, misunderstanding, jealousy or attempt to shirk or escape the maximum duty or losses which may be required."

Every man, he noted, who could be called "a real pilot" was looked up to and appreciated by his fellows.

Early in September the Allied armies struck back hard against the Germans. The Battle of St. Mihiel was followed soon after by the Battle of the Argonne. Both resulted in great victories for the Allies.

American aviation held command of the air throughout the two decisive battles. Mitchell's airmen had three main tasks to accomplish. First, they must provide accurate information for the ground troops. Second, they must prevent enemy air forces from interfering with the Allied air or ground troops. Third, they must bomb areas back of the enemy to stop supplies and hold up any movement along the roads.

These tasks were performed in excellent fashion. After the successful St. Mihiel offensive, General Pershing wrote Mitchell:

"Please accept my sincere congratulations on the successful and very important part taken by the Air Forces under your command in the first offensive of the First American Army. . . .

"Please convey to your command my heartfelt appreciation of their work. I am proud of you all."

Mitchell was deeply gratified to learn that General Trenchard, the British airman he admired so much, had congratulated Pershing on the success of the air operation. The chief of the French air division also spoke of the distinguished leadership Mitchell had provided.

All his planning and hard work were justified. He was repaid for sleepless nights and for endless struggles with higher authority to get the best of planes and equipment for his valiant flying men.

Fittingly, he was promoted to the rank of brigadier general. He also was given a new and higher assignment. He assumed command of the aviation of the Group of Armies. This placed him in charge of the entire Air Service of the American Expeditionary Forces.

The war raced toward its conclusion. The German forces were never able to regain the offensive. Air attacks by Mitchell's fliers against enemy airdromes, supply points, and communications were increasingly effective. German citizens were demanding an end to the war, and there were threats of revolution.

The Germans were beaten. Their leaders knew it.

Finally, on November 11, 1918, the Armistice brought an end to the fighting. All the armies were spared the necessity of carrying the war through the hard winter months.

Mitchell, as he wrote later, "realized that I was pretty tired and that everyone around me felt very much the same way." He added, "I was glad to see the terrific loss of life being stopped."

Four days earlier he had been awarded the Distinguished Service Cross for "repeated acts of extraordinary heroism in action" and for "displaying bravery far beyond that required by his position, . . . setting a personal example to the United States Aviation by piloting his airplane over the battle lines since the entry of the United States into the war."

The citation listed several specific examples of Mitchell's dauntless bravery in action.

The brigadier general, his stars new on his uniform, was at his headquarters in Toul when the Armistice was declared. He did not take long to decide to take a trip into Paris. He must see what was going on there among people who had suffered from war for so long. He set off in his largest automobile, accompanied by several friends.

They soon found that the idea of paying a visit to Paris was shared by many others. The roads into the French capital were choked with automobiles. The cars were filled with singing, shouting men.

"On to Paris!" was the cry of all.

The city itself, when Mitchell and his friends reached it late in the evening, presented a wild scene of excitement and rejoicing.

"Men and women were pulling the captured German cannons, which had lined the streets, up and down the pavements," Mitchell wrote in describing that evening. "Girls, dressed in soldiers' caps and blouses, were going through the drill around the guns that the artillerymen were taught on the front. Everyone was singing, shaking hands, kissing each other, dancing, screaming and yelling—the most spectacular outburst of feeling that I have ever seen."

To the frenzied French civilians every American soldier they saw was a hero. As Mitchell's car, driven by a soldier, proceeded along the street, it was constantly encircled by shouting people. Many jumped up on the car's running board to lean in and embrace the driver.

The streets were so jammed with people that only military vehicles were allowed to proceed. Then the police closed the boulevards to all cars.

Just as a gendarme was telling Mitchell's driver that the street was closed, the American airman was recognized by a group of French pilots who had served under him in the battles of St. Mihiel and the Argonne. They surged toward the car.

"*Vive notre général américain!*" they screamed. "Long live our American general!"

The French policeman was pushed aside as the pilots surrounded Mitchell's automobile. They almost picked it up and carried it down the boulevard. At one time Mitchell counted eighteen of them sitting on the roof of the car, on the radiator, on the mudguards, and all over the back.

Men and women unable to find a place on the car joined hands and formed a ring around it, singing at the top of their voices.

It was a night Billy Mitchell would never forget.

A few days later, he had a long talk with General Pershing. The commander-in-chief told him he was to take the Air Service up to the Rhine River with the Third American Army. This was the force being organized to occupy the territory in that region.

Mitchell remained in Germany until early in January. Then he received notice that he had been asked for by the United States to return there to become Chief of Military Aviation.

Before leaving France he was awarded the French Legion of Honor. He looked up military friends among the British, went to Belgium to see for himself

Commanders and officers of the Allied Forces. France's Marshall Petain (light uniform) in the front row. General Mitchell is directly behind him to his right. General Pershing is at Petain's left.

what had happened there during the war, then visited his sister Ruth in England. Finally he sailed for home.

His ship arrived at New York harbor on February 17, 1919. A group of airplanes from nearby Mitchell Field circled overhead. The airmen were welcoming the homecoming of their hero.

CHAPTER NINE

THE HERO'S WELCOME was followed quickly by disappointment.

First, Mitchell learned that he was not to be chief of Military Aviation at all. He was named assistant chief.

The top position went to an elderly major general named Charles T. Menoher. General Menoher had spent his military life in the cavalry, a branch of the Army which the war had shown to be obsolete. The new head of Military Aviation was not a flier. In fact, it was said he had never been up in a plane.

He was known as a strong disciplinarian—just the man, muttered the non-flying senior officers of the Army and Navy, "to put Billy Mitchell and his flyboys in their place."

Worse to Mitchell than his personal disappointment was the official military attitude toward air power—an attitude, he learned with dismay, of indifference or even ridicule.

The senior staff officers in the War Department saw no need for a national air policy, which Mitchell regarded as vitally necessary. Few of these officers understood the role aviation had played in winning the war. They were graduates of the West Point Military Academy. They looked down on the young fliers who, like Mitchell, had not attended the Academy.

These military traditionalists believed that land armies and battleships alone could provide an adequate national defense.

Mitchell was convinced that aviation inevitably would play a part of the first importance in national defense and in commerce as well. "Only an air force can fight an air force," he declared. "Only an air force can keep ships afloat in war."

He called for the establishment of a single Department of Defense. In this proposed department there would be sub-secretaries for the Air, the Army, and the Navy, all on an equal basis.

Controversy was bound to grow out of these circumstances. It was not long in developing.

A few weeks after Mitchell's return to Washington, he was invited to meet with the general board of the Navy, which was considering what its future aviation policy would be. He went to the meeting with enthusiasm. It seemed to him a wonderful opportunity to convince the fourteen high-ranking naval officers attending the conference that strengthening military aviation was of supreme importance.

He placed before them his proposal for a unified Department of Defense. Shore-based air power was necessary, he said, to protect the coast lines of the United States. Furthermore, he declared it would be possible in the future to make direct attacks on battleships from the air. These giant vessels could not carry enough power to make them invulnerable. Air power, Mitchell maintained, was superior to sea power.

All this was heresy to most of the admirals at the meeting. They listened coldly. Mitchell never received another invitation to appear before the general board.

He sent to the War Department a steady flow of reports, plans, and recommendations for developing military aviation. They were ignored.

He began what was to become a long series of appearances before congressional committees to give evidence showing the need for aviation development.

Committee members heard what he had to say, and some of them appeared sympathetic. But legislative measures to carry out Mitchell's proposals always were buried in the committee. They were never sent to the whole Congress for action.

Assistant Secretary of War Crowell was one man who saw the need for building an airplane manufacturing industry in the United States. The U.S. Air Service had not a single airplane entirely designed and made in America.

Mitchell's hopes soared when a group of military and civilian aviation experts, headed by Crowell, went to Europe to study civil use of aviation. They visited France, Italy, and England. They conferred with government officials, ranking military commanders, and the leading aircraft manufacturers.

This American Aviation Mission reported to the Secretary of War on its return that "immediate action" was necessary to safeguard the air interests of the United States. Otherwise, the report declared, a vitally necessary industry would disappear.

"Ninety percent of the industry created during the war has been liquidated," the Secretary of War was informed. "Unless some definite policy is adopted by the government, the remaining ten percent will also disappear.

"The American Aviation Mission therefore recommends the concentration of all air activities of the United States within the direction of a single government agency, co-equal with the Departments of War, Navy, and Commerce."

Mitchell, who had managed unofficially to obtain a copy of the report, felt his heart beat faster as he read it. Although the members of the mission had gone their separate ways in England and on the continent, they had all independently arrived at the same set of conclusions. They were in full accord.

The Secretary of War, Mitchell told himself, would simply have to act on their recommendation!

But nothing happened. The Secretary accepted the report from his assistant and said he would look it over and make it public in due time. But he did not. The report was never issued as a public document. It was not released to the press. It was suppressed.

An Army officer, familiar with the enmity of the general staff to the proposal for a unified Defense Department, wrote years later that the Crowell report "was promptly thrown into the nearest wastebasket."

More blows to Mitchell came in rapid succession.

The appropriation of $83,000,000 which he had asked Congress to approve for the Air Service was cut to $25,000,000. An order was issued by the Secretary of War that all temporary officers, holding war-time rank, must be discharged from the Air Service. This would leave but 232 officers; only 149 of them were pilots. In nine days 6,000 fliers were discharged.

Some friendly congressmen tried to pass a law to undo the damage, but they were unable to muster much support. Assistant Secretary Crowell resigned in disgust.

The advocates of air power appeared to be defeated at every turn. Mitchell, their leader, had come back from the war with plans for a force of 5,100 planes and an Air Service establishment of 1,923 officers and 21,853 men. He had expected the military to lead the way for development of civilian aviation.

None of his expectations had been realized. The Air Service was being reduced almost to the point of non-existence. No airplanes were being built in the United States. The hidebound ideas of the aging generals and admirals prevailed. Mitchell himself was in very low favor around the War Department.

Naturally, he never thought of giving up the battle.

If he could not get action in Washington, perhaps he could arouse the American people. They could then put pressure on Congress to demand the building of an adequate Air Service. Even the generals and admirals could not stand up against a determined Congress.

So Mitchell reasoned. He set out to make speeches before public gatherings. He planned experiments and demonstrations that would compel Americans to see what aviation meant to the future of their nation and the world.

"The most necessary thing now," he declared, "is to educate the people as to what may be expected in aeronautics and how it affects the well-being of every citizen in this country."

He went to work on this educational project with all his boundless energy. He spoke before all kinds of organizations throughout the country. He had never considered himself an orator, but the message he had to bring rang out eloquently because of his complete belief in what he had to say.

"Our air defense is in such decay that if we went to war tomorrow we would again have to buy our planes from England or France," he told the American people, "or again be in the disgraceful position of having to let our friends hold our enemies off our backs until we can get ready.

"Only by direct and unified control of all branches of aviation, as in England and France, can we have sufficient development."

In England, in December 1919, the first specially designed passenger airliner was put into operation on a daily schedule between London and Paris. A network of passenger airlines was being extended throughout Europe. A blueprint had been laid out to carry this network on into Morocco, India, and other countries.

But the United States stood still.

Billy Mitchell did not stand still. He was constantly on the move, physically and mentally. Words alone, he decided, were not enough to stir the nation as he thought it should be stirred. Something sensational must be done to direct public attention to aviation and what it could do.

He hit on the idea of a transcontinental race by air. On October 4, 1919, it was announced that such a race would be held, starting simultaneously at Long Island, New York, and San Francisco. All Army fliers with planes having a speed of not less than ninety miles per hour would be allowed to participate.

There were no civilian landing fields. Mitchell arranged to make pastures available for landing at twenty control points across the country. To avoid accidents, night flying was prohibited.

On October 11, the race began. Sixty-three fliers started.

Mitchell flew over the takeoff from Long Island. As the racers disappeared in the distance, he landed his plane and told reporters, "This is being done with the idea of seeing how quickly we can shift our aerial force from one coast to the other in case of an attack on either side. With an air service there is no coastline. We will soon be just as liable to attack in the middle states as along the coast."

The transcontinental airplane race was a tremendous success from a popular point of view. At the control points, people turned out by the thousands to see the racing planes land and take off. The newspapers carried daily accounts on their front pages. All across the country, people stopped whatever they were doing to stare into the sky as they heard the sound of airplane engines.

When the race was ended, Lieutenant B. W. Maynard was announced as the winner. He had flown across the continent at the fantastic average speed of 107.45 miles an hour. His actual flying time was 25 hours, 11 minutes, 8½ seconds.

The race did much to awaken Americans to an interest in aviation. This interest was further stimulated by the "barnstorming" fliers who now entered the scene. A "barnstormer" was a flier—most likely one of Mitchell's discharged military pilots—who flew his own plane from one town to another to take up individuals brave enough to try the experience.

The barnstormer used a pasture near the town for his flying field. For a small fee—three dollars, five dollars—he would give citizens their first experience of travel by air. Usually he could accommodate only two passengers per flight.

Exhibition flying also was very popular. County and state fairs engaged daredevil stunt fliers to entertain the people. These fliers "looped the loop," flew upside down, flew with a man crawling out on one wing. They were popular heroes, with their leather flying helmets, their goggles, and their general air of careless bravery.

Lt. W. B. Maynard ready to fly across the Rocky Mountains in the 1919 race.

Mitchell was succeeding in his aim of getting the public interested in aviation. But the effects of this interest on Congress remained to be felt. The United States continued to lag far behind other nations in both military and civilian aviation.

By 1921, there was still not one commercial passenger airline in the country. France, Germany, Spain, Rumania, South Africa, even China and Japan had regular airliners transporting cargo and passengers. But not the United States. There was not even an official in the government charged with the responsibility of developing commercial aviation.

Mitchell's business was military aviation, of course, but he knew that commercial pilots in time of emergency could quickly be shifted to military flying. Commercial aviation would demand airplanes from factories that could, if the need arose, be turned to the production of military aircraft. Commercial and military aviation were linked together. So Mitchell was deeply concerned about the development of both.

He was himself a living example of air power. He traveled a great deal and nearly always by air. In his endless round of public addresses, he would speak in a city, then be hundreds of miles away the next morning.

A newspaper reporter wrote of him: "General

Mitchell has speed written all over him. He talks, thinks, and practices speed. Looking about ten years younger than his actual forty-two, the most competent and intrepid pilot in America is as trim and fit as a college halfback."

The reporter went on to remark that the most remarkable thing of all was that "Pilot Mitchell, with the safe and easy rank of a general, does a second lieutenant's work."

That work was piloting his own plane. He still held to his wartime decision to fly himself whenever possible.

But his real work, that of carrying on his struggle to build air power, was not the work of a second lieutenant.

Despite all the obstacles thrown in his way, he was determined to prove that the United States could no longer afford to look solely to the Navy as its first line of defense. The battleship was a weapon of the past. He and his men and their bombing planes would show this to be true if given an opportunity by the Navy. That was all he asked.

Finally, with great reluctance and driven only by mounting public opinion, Secretary of the Navy Josephus Daniels agreed to give Mitchell the chance he wanted.

CHAPTER TEN

BILLY MITCHELL TOLD a House of Representatives subcommittee on aviation exactly what he proposed:

"Let the Navy turn out a battleship, destroyer, supply ship, and scout cruiser. Air officers will go so far as to be willing to let the Navy use every anti-aircraft device they want, with service ammunition, on the ships, provided we can bomb them. All we want is to demonstrate before congressional bodies so that they will be able to judge for themselves."

Having agreed to provide ex-German warships as targets for the bombing experiments, Navy officials proceeded to make the tests as difficult as possible for the airmen.

The Navy set all the rules. Strict limits were placed on the number of hits allowed and the caliber

Aerial view of Langley Field, Virginia, 1921.

of the missiles to be used. Worse, from Mitchell's point of view, was the naval command's insistence that the target ships must be anchored in deep water 75 miles out to sea. This would place them 100 miles from Langley Field, takeoff point for the fliers.

Mitchell contended that with the kind of planes available this distance gave rise to unnecessary danger. He did not see why the ships to be bombed should be so far away from the shore.

"It was up to us, however," he said resignedly, "to show what we advocated could be done, so we had to accept the conditions that were offered."

Plans moved forward to conduct the tests in June and July 1921. But before the time arrived

Mitchell became involved in a controversy that almost forced him out of his post as assistant chief of Military Aviation.

Six airplanes flying from Langley Field to Washington ran into an electric storm. Mitchell, flying alone in a small plane, said later it was the worst storm he had ever seen. One of the large planes in the group, carrying seven men, crashed in Maryland. All the men were killed.

Mitchell made a scorching statement to the press that this disaster might have been avoided if there had been a radio service to provide flying directions and weather bulletins to pilots. He did not stop with that. Greater efficiency and safety were possible, he said. But they could be brought about only by the establishment of a unified Defense Department in which equal status was given Navy, Army, and Air branches.

His argument was an old one to Mitchell. This time, however, following the worst airplane disaster the nation had known, it attracted widespread public attention. Newspapers and aviation publications echoed his cry for a better and safer Air Service—and, some were quick to suggest, with Billy Mitchell as its head.

Such talk did not meet with approval in high

military quarters. Before this time Mitchell had been scolded and reprimanded by the War Department for speaking his mind too freely. Now the word "insubordination," which is a grave charge in the Army, began to be used against him. Some Army and Navy officers joined forces to whip up sentiment against Mitchell in the War Department.

The admirals and generals who ran the Army and the Navy were not unpatriotic or dishonorable men. Of course not. They were as sincere in their conviction that the old ways were best as Mitchell was in his that sweeping changes must be made.

The old Navy officers could not conceive of a time when their branch of the service would not be the nation's first line of defense. The old Army officers felt their branch would be seriously downgraded if the Air Service were made co-equal with the Army. So they combined their efforts against the upstart.

Early in June, General Menoher, chief of Military Aviation, made a formal request to Secretary of War Weeks that Mitchell be removed from office. Weeks told a newspaper reporter that he probably would comply with the request. He said that "all precedents of Army discipline and service" favored such a step.

When this statement was published, it brought

a renewed uproar on editorial pages and among aeronautical organizations throughout the country. Resolutions were passed supporting Mitchell. Rumors spread that if he lost his office, the planned bombing tests would never be held.

Weeks was forced by the public clamor to back down. He announced that the bombing tests would go on as scheduled. He quietly induced Menoher to withdraw his request that Mitchell be removed. He gave the airman a mild official reprimand and asked him to stop talking so much.

The tests were conducted under the observation of a joint Army-Navy board of officers. They occupied the control ship, from which orders governing the bombing were to come. Another naval transport carried high government officials, other military officers, many members of Congress, and a large group of newspaper correspondents.

Mitchell was satisfied with the audience. He was especially interested in the presence of the congressmen and the news writers. He wanted the lawmakers to see what bombing could do, and he wanted the world to know the story from the press.

The first two tests were carried out by naval fliers. Bombs from Navy seaplanes sank a large ex-German submarine with 12 bombs in 16 minutes.

They were less successful with their next target, an old U.S. battleship. The naval aircraft dropped a total of 80 dummy bombs. But only two direct hits were scored.

"Wait until *my* fliers get into action," Mitchell said.

They had their chance on July 21. Mitchell himself led his air brigade in an attack on a former German destroyer set adrift at sea 100 miles from Langley Field. The Army fliers sank the vessel in 19 minutes, using 44 bombs.

Next came the bombing of a bigger ship, the *Frankfurt*, a cruiser captured from the Germans. Mitchell fumed at the conditions laid down for this test. Ten alternating Army and Navy attacks were to be made. A rule was issued that in the first six attacks only light bombs, weighing 250 and 300 pounds, could be used. No bombs heavier than 600 pounds would be allowed in the last four attacks.

Mitchell did not think the lighter bombs would sink the *Frankfurt*. He was right. After each attack, time was taken out for official observers to come aboard and inspect the damage. Although the cruiser was hit repeatedly by the light bombs, only the deck and superstructure were wrecked. The cruiser remained afloat and seaworthy.

132

Bombing of the *Frankfurt.*

The senior officers on the observation ship rejoiced. If it was that hard to get the 5,100-ton *Frankfurt* to the bottom of the sea, Mitchell's bombers would never be able to sink a battleship. So they told one another and the accompanying newsmen.

Their rejoicing came too soon. Late in the afternoon the first attack by six army bombers carrying 600-pound bombs began. Fourteen bombs were dropped in a little more than ten minutes. The attack blasted the cruiser and the hopes of the naval officers. Within little more than half an hour after the attack was launched, the *Frankfurt* went down.

Next a battleship! Mitchell knew the crucial test was at hand. As he afterward said, "We had already proved that we could sink any other ship except a battleship. Still, all this would be forgotten if we failed to kill, bury, and cover up the *Ostfriesland*."

General Mitchell (center) inspecting the effects of a 300-lb. bomb's explosion on the deck of a battleship.

That was the name of the giant of the seas which was to be the target of the final experiment. The *Ostfriesland* was the former flagship of one of Germany's battle fleets. It was a 27,000-ton vessel. Some observers had called this an unsinkable ship. It was divided into many watertight compartments. Some might be destroyed, but others would keep the *Ostfriesland* afloat.

Mitchell disagreed. His fliers, in a superb state of training, were excitedly determined that bombs from their planes would send the mighty ship down into the briny deep.

That was exactly what happened on July 21. As the unbelieving admirals watched from their observation ship, the *Ostfriesland* went down after 21½ minutes of attack from Mitchell's bombers. The sea power men were disconsolate; some wept as the great gray battleship disappeared from sight. But the air power men were jubilant.

"As we returned to Langley Field," Mitchell wrote, "all the planes and airships of our brigade were in the air, and the cannons on the ground were booming. All the officers, their families, and the mechanics of the squadrons, who by their tireless attention night and day had enabled us to remain in the air and do our work, were there."

It was a day of triumph.

An editorial in the *New York Times* said the need for a strong air force had been proved to be more important than going ahead with a program of building heavy battleships.

"The achievement was a great triumph," said the *Times*, "for the intelligent, strong-willed, persistent assistant chief of the Army Air Service, a leader who asks no subordinate to take a greater risk than he is willing to take himself."

But if Billy Mitchell thought the battle was over, he was wrong.

He eagerly awaited the official report from the joint Army-Navy board. When it came in August, it proved to be a sharp disappointment.

This report, signed by General Pershing, which added to the bitterness of the blow to Mitchell, admitted that aircraft bombing could sink or damage "any naval vessel at present constructed." But then it went on to the conclusion that "the battleship is still the backbone of the fleet and the bulwark of the nation's sea defense."

Mitchell had already made his own report to General Menoher. His conclusions were in direct opposition to those of the joint board. He struck out sharply at the "desk admirals" who opposed the development of air power. And he once again renewed his call for establishment of a unified Department of Defense.

Mitchell's report at first was filed away without being made public. But friends were determined that it should not be buried, and it soon reached the press. Sensational headlines told of a new chapter in the controversy over air power.

Menoher had enough of the fight. He resigned. A strong public demand went up for Mitchell to be named as his replacement. But the command of the Air Service went instead to Colonel Mason W. Patrick, who was promptly promoted to major general. Patrick was an officer in the Corps of Engineers—and a non-flier. Mitchell stayed on as his assistant.

He bravely maintained that he did not care about titles. He still had his job to do, he told his friends, and he would do it to the best of his ability.

He headed another mission to Europe to study aviation developments in that area. After three months abroad, he came home with extensive recommendations for the U.S. Air Service.

Although the War Department and the Navy wanted to muzzle him, he made dozens of speeches before various organizations. The usual theme of his talks was summed up in an address at a banquet given in his honor by the 1922 Aeronautical Congress.

"Air power must be put on an equal footing with land and sea power," he repeated doggedly. "We must have a united Department of Defense. We cannot have the urgently necessary development of aviation in this country under the present complete lack of policy."

He sounded this theme also in magazine articles. He had been ordered by Secretary Weeks not to say anything in print before submitting his statements to the War Department for approval. But there was no way to silence Mitchell on a subject he considered of vital concern to the nation.

He flew around the country on inspection missions. It was with dismay that he reported the results of his inspections. In El Paso, Texas, he found the air squadron to be in "just as poor condition as can be and still called an observation squadron." Along the Canadian border, he reported, the whole effective air force of the Army was made up of 15 pursuit planes.

The air establishment of the United States was steadily going down. This was happening even as his airmen were setting one new world's record after another. Such records, Mitchell pointed out, were not worth much if the flying equipment was so sparse and so far behind that of European nations.

He kept up his own flying, and on October 18, 1922, established a new speed record of 224.38 miles an hour in an air meet. A little less than 43 years of age, Billy Mitchell was speed king of the air.

He managed to get authority to carry out a new experiment in bombing battleships. In September 1923, his planes swooped down on two old battleships built in 1906. They were 441 feet long, each of 15,000 tons. The first was sunk in only 27 minutes. Not much longer was required to send down the second.

To Mitchell the test seemed a great success. But General Pershing, his old commander, gave a statement to the press which said, "Tests do not prove modern warships can be sunk by bombers."

The assistant chief of the Air Service wondered angrily what proof would be required.

Pressures mounted on him, personal as well as professional. His first marriage had ended in divorce after the war. His beloved mother, who had come to Washington to make a home for him, had died late in 1922. Nothing was left to him but his crusade for air power.

Still, Mitchell was not a man to sit around and mope. While on a trip to Selfridge Field, Michigan, he was taken by a friend to a horse show. There he met a young woman named Elizabeth Miller. She was riding in the show. It was natural that Mitchell, with his fondness for horses, should fall into conversation with her about riding.

Soon he was taking the attractive girl on airplane rides. Betty Miller had never been up before, and at first she was frightened. She got over that and began to enjoy flying with the best pilot in the country. Betty and Mitchell found that they liked to do the same things, especially such outdoor sports as riding, hunting, and skiing.

Mitchell's gay spirit reasserted itself. It was matched by her own gaiety. They fell deeply in love, and on October 11, 1923, they were married. Mitchell felt that he had never been happier.

Twelve days after their wedding, the couple set out on a round-the-world journey that lasted nine months. It was a dream trip, taking them to Hawaii, the Philippines, China, India, the Dutch East Indies, Siam, Korea, Japan—the far places of the earth.

Honeymoon though it was, Mitchell was at work. His keen eyes looked to the future defense of the United States, especially against a possible attack from Japan. Air power was sadly lacking. There was little coordination between the Army and Navy.

In Hawaii, he reported, "The commanding general of the Army and the commanding admiral of the Navy would not even go to the same social functions together. I have never seen anything like it. Each claimed to be the senior officer."

He found strong anti-American feeling in Japan. Regarding air power, he warned: "It takes no longer to teach Japanese to fly than it does Anglo-Saxons. One oftens hears it said that the Japanese cannot fly. Nothing is more fallacious than this. They can fly, are going to fly, and may end up by developing the greatest air power in the world."

General and Mrs. Mitchell in Siam on their 1923 tour of the Far East.

Back in the United States, Mitchell plunged into writing magazine articles and testifying before congressional committees about the threat he saw facing the nation.

Germany, forbidden to rearm by the treaty ending World War I, was establishing aeronautical enterprises in other countries. In Italy, the dictator Benito Mussolini was building up the air force. In Japan, seventeen aircraft factories were "going full blast and some running night shifts."

In the United States, Mitchell noted glumly, not

a single aircraft factory was employed to its capacity. In fact, in the year 1924, American military aviation was sliding down to nothingness. Some air squadrons were placed on the inactive list. Others were substantially reduced in strength.

Mitchell knew that this combination of facts spelled great danger for the United States. He resolved to make a last desperate effort, at whatever cost to himself, to arouse the country and the Congress to the danger.

He went before a special congressional investigating committee to accuse Army and Naval witnesses of falsifying the facts about air power. Their purpose, he boldly charged, was to deceive the country and to deceive Congress. He presented evidence to prove his charge.

As the investigation went on, Secretary Weeks threatened Mitchell with demotion—even with court martial—unless he halted his testimony. Telegrams angrily protesting this threat poured into Washington.

Naval officials appeared before the committee to sneer at the results of the battleship bombings. There were exceptions. Several admirals came to Mitchell's defense. One, who had witnessed all the bombings, declared, "General Mitchell has done more

President Calvin Coolidge inspecting General Mitchell's plane.

to demonstrate the power of air attack than the general board of the Navy and all the admirals combined."

But it was no use. From President Calvin Coolidge came the pronouncement that the battleships had been "fully vindicated." There would be no change in the nation's defense policy.

Punishment must be meted out to the rebel. Mitchell's wartime rank of brigadier general was taken away. He reverted to his permanent rank of colonel—although to his friends and to the American people he remained General Billy Mitchell.

Colonel Mitchell was reassigned to Fort Sam Houston in Texas. He was given no duties there. He had been banished.

CHAPTER ELEVEN

"THE QUESTION of what happens to me is a small matter," Mitchell said of the treatment accorded him. "The question of reorganization of our defense system is a big matter."

He fired his biggest gun yet after two air disasters early in September 1925—and, figuratively speaking, the walls came tumbling down.

As an answer to Mitchell's charge that it was doing nothing about air power, the Navy staged a flight from San Francisco to Honolulu. To save money, the planes were provided only with enough fuel to get them across if the winds were right. The winds changed and were unfavorable.

Only one pilot tried to go the entire distance. His plane ran out of gasoline 300 miles from Hawaii.

The plane crashed into the sea with its pilot and crew of four.

Nine days passed and the five men were given up for lost. Miraculously, however, they were picked up by rescuers as they navigated their seaplane toward land.

Even before their rescue, the nation was rocked by an even greater air disaster. This was the breaking up and crashing during an electrical storm of the Navy dirigible, the *Shenandoah*. Thirteen men were killed.

The nationwide tour of the *Shenandoah* also had been planned by the Navy as part of its effort to show that air power was being given due attention, no matter what such critics as Mitchell said. It was a flight for publicity purposes.

The *Shenandoah* was an old airship. Mitchell had warned that it was unsafe and should be scrapped. The commander of the craft had protested the order to take her on the tour. But he was commanded to proceed.

To the stunned American people, Secretary of the Navy Wilbur incredibly stated that the disasters showed the nation had nothing to fear from air power. In view of the failure of the Hawaiian flight and the crash of the *Shenandoah*, he said, "We have come to

The wreck of the *Shenandoah*.

the conclusion that the Atlantic and Pacific are still our best defense."

At his remote post in Texas, Mitchell raged inwardly. Newspaper reporters converged on his office. They wanted comment on the disasters from the leading American proponent of air power.

"Wait," he told them.

He closeted himself in his office to work out what he wanted to say. He labored on the statement for a full day and night. At five o'clock in the morning of September 5, he came out to the waiting reporters.

To them he said he had been asked from all parts of the country to give his opinion about the reasons for the disasters. He gave it bluntly:

"These accidents are the result of the incompetency, the criminal negligence, and the almost treasonable administration of our national defense by the Navy and War Departments."

He had a written statement 6,000 words long. As the reporters fell upon the copies made available to them, Mitchell predicted that by Monday he would be under arrest to face a court martial. He spoke on Saturday.

In his long statement, Mitchell summed up what he had been saying for years about the obstinate refusal of the military bureaucracy to see the need for building national air power. He said that witnesses sent by the Army and Navy to testify before the congressional committee gave incomplete, misleading, or false information about aeronautics. Airmen themselves were afraid to speak out because frankness on the subject could ruin their careers.

"As far as I personally am concerned," his statement ended, "I am looking for no advancement in any service. I have had the finest career that any man could have in the armed service of our United States.

"I owe the government everything—the government owes me nothing. As a patriotic American citizen, I can stand by no longer and see these disgusting performances by the Navy and War Departments, at the expense of the lives of our people and the delusion of the American public."

The statement was the most bitter criticism of the high command ever voiced by any United States military officer.

Monday morning, just as Mitchell had predicted, newspaper headlines blazed the story that the War Department planned a court martial for the plainspoken colonel.

It was set for October 28, 1925. The charge was violation of the 98th Article of War. This military regulation, known in the armed service as the "grab bag article," provides punishment for any "conduct of a nature to bring discredit upon the military service."

Mitchell was recalled to Washington. He was technically under arrest, but of course he was not imprisoned. The country would not have stood for that.

Court martial of an officer of Mitchell's rank and eminence was a drastic undertaking. The trial, which lasted more than six weeks, created a sensation throughout the country. The dingy courtroom was crowded daily with news reporters and photographers.

They were largely in sympathy with Mitchell, and their daily reports clearly showed the bias of the court, which was composed of nine general officers and one colonel.

It quickly became evident that the court was determined to put every possible obstacle in the way of Mitchell's civilian lawyer. The accused wanted the issue to be whether he had been telling the truth about the state of the nation's air power. But the prosecution wanted to avoid that question, concentrating instead on the charge that Mitchell had repeatedly violated army discipline by his attacks on official policy.

Under this procedure, Mitchell would have to be found guilty of violating discipline even if his charges were determined to be true!

One witness after another, including many of the nation's leading airmen, appeared to back up what Mitchell had said so often about the military bureaucracy's failure to develop air power. The famed World War I Ace, Eddie Rickenbacker, was a witness for Mitchell. So were Major Carl Spaatz and Major H. H. Arnold, both of whom later were major figures in the Air Corps. They supported Mitchell's charge that high officers gave false information to Congress when they knew the truth.

The young widow of the dead commander of the *Shenandoah* testified for Mitchell. She charged that the judge advocate of the board of inquiry into the death of the airship had tried to influence her testimony before the board.

Fiorello LaGuardia, a fiery congressman from New York, testified that the city could be effectively attacked from the air if its only protection was by anti-aircraft defense. He strongly backed Mitchell's claim that a fighting air force was vitally necessary for effective defense.

A mass of evidence was produced by such witnesses to substantiate Mitchell's charge that "the people put their trust in the War and Navy depart-

Col. Mitchell at his court martial. Mrs. Mitchell is seated at his left.

ments to give the country adequate defenses, and they have not done so." He himself was on the witness stand three full days.

Through the press the American people followed the trial in a high state of excitement. Crowds stormed the courtroom every day, making it clear they were on Mitchell's side. Leading newspapers predicted Mitchell's acquittal.

But the judges were not concerned with public opinion and not even deeply interested in the evidence. The order for this court martial was understood to have come from President Coolidge himself. That was enough for most of them. Besides, here was an opportunity to put down this insubordinate upstart for all time.

Mitchell foresaw the outcome. When the time came for him or his counsel to make a final summing up, he stood in front of the assembled court and spoke quietly.

"The truth of every statement I have made has been proved by good and sufficient evidence," he said, "by actual fliers who have gained their knowledge firsthand in war and peace.

"The evidence before this court bears out in its entirety the fact that our Air Service, as I testified, has only nine planes fit for war and that all the others are obsolete and many dangerous.

"The court has refrained from ruling whether the truth in this case constitutes an absolute defense or not.

"To proceed further with the case would serve no useful purpose. I have therefore directed my counsel to close my part of the proceeding without further argument."

He sat down. The judges looked at one another in surprise. Then they filed out to consider their verdict. Two hours and 54 minutes later they returned.

The verdict was guilty on all counts.

Mitchell was sentenced to five years' suspension from rank, command, and pay. The Secretary of War recommended that the sentence be modified to grant half of his pay and allowances "during the pleasure of the President."

On January 26, 1926, President Coolidge confirmed the sentence and approved the recommended modification. He also spoke severely of Mitchell's "defiance toward his military superiors."

Two days later, Mitchell tendered his resignation as an officer of the United States Army.

CHAPTER TWELVE

BILLY MITCHELL was just forty-five years of age when he left the Army he had served all his adult life. But he was tired—worn out by the struggle against odds which in the end he was unable to overcome. His brave heart had been strained by the pressures brought against him and the controversies in which he had no choice but to become involved.

Naturally, he had no thought of giving up his fight for the development of air power in the United States.

"From now on," he said, "I feel I can better serve my country and the flag I love by bringing a realization of the true conditions of our national defense straight to the people than by remaining muzzled in the Army."

He had bought a home, "Boxwood," near Middle-
burg, Virginia. Here he and his wife could engage in
the outdoor activities so pleasing to them both. They
raised fine horses and pedigreed dogs. They hunted
and fished in the woods and streams. He built a
cabin cruiser which proved a source of great pleasure
to him and his wife.

Boxwood was his refuge and retreat, but it was at
the same time his base of operations in carrying forward the campaign for air power. He poured out
magazine articles and books. He made plans for a
University of Aviation to be financed by private funds,

Billy Mitchell jumping at a horse show.

for he knew the government would not finance it. Finally he gave up this idea. They would only think, he said sadly, he was trying to promote himself.

War was coming, he warned America again and again. He himself had seen the Japanese getting ready for armed conflict. He realized that they had observers at his bombing tests in 1921. At his court martial, several Japanese had been busily making notes and taking pictures. They knew the sorry state of American air power.

Whenever war came, it would be air power that dominated the Pacific. In Europe, Germany was building a mighty air force.

Yet the United States remained unprepared for self-defense. Military unification was essential.

So went Mitchell's warnings. He had many supporters in Congress, in the press and among the people generally. But then came the hard times of the early 1930's. People had to think about getting enough to eat and keeping their homes. These personal problems were immediate and pressing. The threat of war seemed far-off and unreal.

Nevertheless, Mitchell persisted in his crusade. He appeared again before congressional committees to urge the development of long-distance bombing planes. He was cheered by reports in the press that

President Franklin D. Roosevelt, who took office in 1933, would sponsor basic reforms in the national defense system.

It was said, in particular, that Roosevelt would press for unification of government aviation operations. A new aviation organization reportedly was being worked out. Friendly congressmen and others urgently recommended that Mitchell be made head of the proposed organization.

But the call did not come. A presidential commission was appointed to study the question of air power. Mitchell was not even named to the commission.

All the disappointments, the hard schedule of speaking and writing, and the emotion he poured into his drive to arouse the country took their toll at last. Mitchell said himself that he had "suddenly grown old," although he was only 56.

In January 1936, after attending the funeral of his old commander, General Greely, he developed pneumonia. A few days later, he entered a New York hospital. There, on February 19, 1936, the stout heart stopped beating.

Many men who had scorned Billy Mitchell's warnings that the United States faced great danger lived to see his fears come true. In Europe in the early 1940's, the brave combat forces resisted German attack against heavy odds while the United States frantically built up its forces. Japan bombed Pearl Harbor, Hawaii, on December 7, 1941, destroying the U.S. battle fleet.

World War II proved conclusively that Billy Mitchell had been right—completely right all along. His writings on air power had been translated and published abroad, to be studied by those who soon were to be the enemies of the United States. At home he was punished for holding out boldly for his ideas.

In addition to his military vision, Mitchell made great contributions to flying safety. Many aeronautic inventions and procedures now common in flying are directly traceable to him.

Billy Mitchell's dream of a unified U.S. Department of Defense became a reality after the war. He was a man ahead of his time. His name will live forever on the Roll of Honor of American patriots.

BIBLIOGRAPHY

GAVREAU, EMILE HENRY and COHEN, LESTER. *Billy Mitchell Founder of Our Air Force and Prophet Without Honor.* New York, E. P. Dutton and Co., 1942.

HURLEY, ALFRED F. *Billy Mitchell: Crusader for Air Power.* New York, Franklin Watts, Inc., 1964.

LEVINE, ISAAC DON. *Mitchell Pioneer of Air Power,* rev. ed. New York, Duell, Sloane & Pearce, 1958.

MITCHELL, BILLY. "Billy Mitchell in Alaska." *American Heritage,* Vol. 12 (February, 1961).

————. *Memoirs of World War I: From Start to Finish of Our Greatest War.* New York, Random House, Inc., 1960.

MITCHELL, RUTH. *My Brother Bill: The Life of General "Billy" Mitchell.* New York, Harcourt, Brace, 1953.

PATRICK, MASON M. *The United States in the Air.* Garden City, N. Y., Doubleday, Doran & Co., 1928.

INDEX